'Anderson writes with a combination of guarded introspection and detachment ... he conjures a cracked and confused persona, fumbling his way through a bizarre early adulthood, by turns gleefully hedonistic and wantonly self-destructive, hardworking and profligate, egotistical and insecure, a character more likely to be seen shuffling around in a dressing-grown smoking fags and staring out the window than prancing on the stage ... *Afternoons with the Blinds Drawn* is another milestone in a flourishing latterday career' *Guardian*

'A compelling personal account of the dramas of a singular British band' Neil Tennant

'Honest and lyrical ... Anderson, in his lyrics, has always been fantastic at capturing the sleaze of underground city living and he does the same here ... Anderson's writing is as he is in real life: sharp, unsparing and sensitive' Miranda Sawyer, *Observer*

'You're unlikely to read another music autobiography quite as honestly reflective as this one' *Sunday Express*

'Thanks to his thoughtful analysis of those wild times, *Afternoons with the Blinds Drawn* lets in a lot of light' Victoria Segal, *Sunday Times*

'The story of Suede's rise and fall, the drugs and the feuds with other bands isn't pretty, but Anderson is on typically sharp form as he tells it' *Telegraph*

'Anderson stopped his enchanting first memoir, *Coal Black Mornings*, just short of the band's brilliant early 1990s breakthrough. Here, he handles their operatic rise and fall with the same thoughtful grace, picking through the paraphernalia of addiction, fame and ego with self-lacerating honesty and a lyrical eye for time and place' *Sunday Times*

'Poetic atmosphere (and good writing) are favoured over dirty detail' *The Times*

AFTERNOONS WITH THE BLINDS DRAWN

BRETT ANDERSON

ABACUS

First published in Great Britain in 2019 by Little, Brown
This paperback edition published in 2020 by Abacus

1 3 5 7 9 10 8 6 4 2

A CIP catalogue record for this book
is available from the British Library.

ISBN 978-0-349-14364-4

Typeset in Granjon by M Rules
Printed and bound in Great Britain by
Clays Ltd, Elcograf S.p.A.

Papers used by Abacus are from well-managed forests
and other responsible sources.

Abacus
An imprint of
Little, Brown Book Group
Carmelite House
50 Victoria Embankment
London EC4Y 0DZ

An Hachette UK Company
www.hachette.co.uk

www.littlebrown.co.uk

For my family

CONTENTS

PART ONE

THE BOOK I SAID I WOULDN'T WRITE

The peeling walls of the tiny bathroom were crumbling and flaking from the damp eating into the plasterwork and a small patch of mildew was spreading its delicate filigree of greying fungus across the coving like a little hand-painted forest. A mean-looking slatted window peered out on to the black sealant roof of the side return, and beyond that it was possible to glimpse the rows of brick houses that backed on to the scruffy weed-strewn gardens; dumping grounds for rusted old bicycles and rotary dryers and abandoned bits of furniture. Between the patches of mould dampened badly scissored random images were stuck to the crumbling paintwork with little discs of Blu-Tack and inside the cracked shallow bath a terrapin skittered and scurried around the parabolic enamel walls of his prison in a sorry circling dance.

The bathroom door opened on to a tiny lightless corridor which in turn led into a high-ceilinged cor-niced room, its walls merging and shimmering as the flickering shadows made by the candles twirled and the flames guttered. The rattling loosely fitted floor-to-ceiling windows gazed out over a wrought-iron balcony and on to the stucco facades of Moorhouse Road in Notting Hill, the occasional twinkling glim-mer of a kitchen light betraying the presence of the odd night owl adrift in their own private nocturnal rituals. Strange-looking glass beads hung from the door lintels and drying, browning artichokes sat for-gotten in a cracked china bowl on a small side table next to the scruffy slate-grey sofa, and scattered all around us were half-empty bottles and torn Rizla packets and ash-trays heaving with butts. The night had been a long one. My old friend Alan and I had spent most of it smoking and chattering excitedly and listening to a cassette demo of 'To The Birds', rewinding and rewinding until the ceremony became a frenzy of looping indulgence as we sat lost in our own private meandering thoughts and the neighbours groaned and thumped and covered their ears with their pillows. The world was slowly shifting, our lives were realigning and beyond the dreary mundanity we could glimpse a different future, something that sparkled with promise and possibility, and sensing this we would sit for hours, listening and nattering and plotting and planning and hoping, feeling the knot of anticipation coil tightly within us.

So here I sit writing the book I said I wouldn't write, talking about the things I said I didn't want to talk about. I suppose it was inevitable. I wonder what dragged me to this place beyond a childish need to be heard, a somewhat garish impulse to tell the world my story. On the countless early mornings I spent lying staring at the ceiling thinking about this the one thing I promised myself was that I would again try not to write the same book that we've all read so many times before. Most rock bands tend to follow the same predictable trudge along the same predictable roads through the same predictable check-points, as preordained as the life cycle of a frog or something and so the tale is always going to have an air of inevitability, especially when everyone knows what happens in the last chapter. So instead what I'm going to try to do in these pages is to use elements of my own story as a way to reach out and reveal the broader picture, to look at my journey from struggle to success and to self-destruction and back again and use that narrative to talk about some of the forces that acted on me and to maybe uncover some sort of truth about the machinery that whirrs away, often unseen, especially by those on whom it is working, to create the bands that people hear on the radio. This might seem a little ambitious but it's my way of trying to claim some sort of ownership over the second part of my story, a story that was so assiduously documented by the media and which certainly doesn't need another retelling in that conventional form. It's remarkable how hindsight can lend a clarity that at the time was beyond you. Now I am able to look at what happened to me during the crazed rollercoaster of those salad days and almost see it all happening to someone else, whereas back then it felt so incredibly personal, so utterly immersive, my face pressed up against the glass as it were, far too close to it to be able to see any truth. This, then, is not so much an extension of the scruffy, dog-eared *Bildungsroman* of the first part of my story but instead a different kind of tale, something that pokes and prods at the cogs and gears that have ground around me over the years and hopefully answers a few questions, as much for myself as anyone, as to what exactly happened and why.

And so as the nineties lurched and spluttered into their fledgling years Suede emerged, blinking, from the debris of our rented rooms, dusting ourselves off from the threadbare chaos of our lives and from the scenes of quiet ruin that inspired those early songs. Ours however was to be the longest ever 'overnight success'. I once described our career arc as being like 'a pram that's been pushed down a hill' and it still seems like a fitting metaphor. It has always felt somehow precarious and out of control and ever-so-slightly ter-rifying. I suppose the 'child' in the pram was the four of us, screaming against the bitter slap of the wind as we tumbled into the traffic.

Of course before we picked up speed there were still many awkward evenings standing on stages trying to convince muttering crowds in back rooms of pubs and places like the Camden Underworld and the Islington Powerhaus – confrontations with seas of folded arms and grim, resolute black-jeaned armies wearing 'impress me' faces – but once the tipping point had been reached there was a sense that we could almost at last surrender to the thrilling inevitability of the ride that was pulling us along and that it had started to become something that was bigger than us. I don't mean to say that there was anything approaching a 'scene' yet because there wasn't – our momentum was still our own and it felt that if we were in any vanguard then we were in a vanguard of one. Music history has slightly rewritten itself over the years in that heed-less way that it sometimes does in order to make the pieces of the past fit the truths of the present. On we staggered from stage to stage with holes in our shoes and a tangle of badly dyed hair smelling of Batiste dry shampoo and the musky, cloying bouquet of dead people's clothes and slowly we began to piece together the brittle foundations on which all bands must build the edifice of their work – the fan base. This was years before social media when word of mouth meant literally just that, when the only way to 'make it' was to get out there and play, pressing your sweating flesh against that of the front row, feeling the oily squirm of clammy palms and the report of the stage against the seat of your worn-out needlecords. Gingerly we started to cast our net outside London, for the first time chugging along the motorways in rented off-white Ford Transits to places like the Tunbridge Wells Rumble Club and the Brighton Zap. In those days travel, no matter how humble or prosaic, was still novel and so the journeys rattling around smoking Silk Cut and eating service-station sandwiches as our friend Charlie Charlton barrelled us along the M23 felt like some sort of wonderful adventure. We used to have a fusty old mattress in the back of the van on which we would sit and jabber excitedly on the way there and drink cheap red wine and collapse on the way back while Mat sat up the front with Charlie lighting cigarettes and trying to keep him awake. For young men in their twenties there's something thrillingly virile and tribal about being in a band and in that winsome period before the joylessness of repetition set in there was a powerful sense of belonging; it felt by very definition *outré*, like you were somehow getting away with it. We orbited from sound check to sound check around satellite towns and ring roads living on a diet of Walkers crisps and nicotine as the low frenzy began to build.

Between shows Saul at Nude Records had booked us in at Protocol Studios in north London with a producer called Ed Buller to record our first proper EP which we'd planned to be a double A-side leading with 'The Drowners' and 'To The Birds' and backed up by 'My Insatiable One'. He'd heard some demos and loved them and then had come to see us live and flattered us suitably, choosing to interpret what we were doing as being akin to the beloved pantheon of seventies rock with which he'd grown up. Ed was a producer cast in the old-school mould – a passionate, single-minded, often eccentric figure who would cram himself into tight black suits and stomp around the control room wrapped in scarves and long coats opining wildly like a caricature of a mad composer or the Doctor Who that never was. Over the course of the session he guided us and shaped us and ushered us into the unfamiliar playground of the studio in his warm, avuncular way, peppering the day with hilarious asides and in-jokes that knitted us all together as a team and laid the foundations for a relationship that would end up spanning decades. On the vast spectrum that defines the role of a producer Ed's special skill lies in dealing with people and especially in inspiring the bands with whom he works. He's one of those who makes you feel secure and held. I always felt that working with Suede was for him more than just another job, that he understood that we saw him as part of our bizarre little family – the stable dad to our errant sons. He knew how to rally us and goad us into action, understanding the limits of our elasticity and pushing us just within its breaking point, steering us to what would become our defining work. In teasing out the more seventies rock elements to our sound I think he was instrumental in how we came to be perceived by the music press. In the hands of another producer the visceral, belligerent edge that the band were developing live might have been given more weight and we might have been cast in the more 'alternative' mould. We were very much party to that decision though as it was our wild-eyed and somewhat lofty mission to create music that pushed beyond the narrow margins of the indie ghetto. Still flushed with the arrogance of youth we desperately wanted to define ourselves as something apart from what was at the time a grey morass of under-achievers.

For those who don't know or who have forgotten I think it's important to understand the landscape into which Suede first surfaced. I don't think it would be unfair to say that alternative music at the time had reached a nadir. The indefinite hiatus of the Stone Roses and the dead end of the shoe-gazing movement had created a vacuum into which was sucked a motley mess of ambitionless long-forgotten bands who dressed in shorts and sounded like students – awful worthy acts who prided themselves on their dull indie creden-tials and their sixth-form politics. I know I'm probably in danger of coming across as waspish and unpleasant and my feelings are possibly a little disproportionate but it felt like we were honour-bound to supplant them and that they provided us with a sort of model to react against. Every new wave of bands disparages the last and in a way it's their duty to kill them off in a kind of Oedipal sense. This act of 'patricide' is necessary to distance themselves as a form of self-definition, like a microcosm of the generational conflict that pop music used to be so effective at instilling; an ongoing continuum of death and rebirth. We wanted to be everything those bands weren't – vulnerable, kinetic, ambitious and arch – and we poured the tenets of this manifesto into those three songs on *The Drowners* EP. The budgets were modest which meant that the sessions were fairly basic. Despite our idealism we were still a young band and Ed knew he had to capture something of that raw pulse so despite a couple of vocal and guitar overdubs and a cello and some bongos 'The Drowners' didn't deviate much from its live incarnation. I think those touches were extremely well judged by Ed though and brought out a lilt and a lift to the song which made it for me one of the best-sounding things we ever recorded. 'To The Birds' suffered a little from the classic naivety of a band in the studio for the first time as we were unable to resist adding a kind of sequenced guitar loop which rendered the new version less primal than it should have been. To be honest, 'My

Insatiable One' was a bit of an afterthought. It wasn't until the record was released and the song started gathering attention in the press and cover versions by Morrissey that we belatedly realised what a gem it was. I had been aware that he had been to a couple of early shows and someone had even muttered that they thought they had seen him scribbling notes into a jotter at the back of the Camden Palace during our set. Whether he was learning the words to the song or not is debatable but it made it no less of a shock when one day while shuffling my way around Portobello Market one of the stall-holders selling boot-leg cassettes sidled up to me and pressed a tape recording from a Swiss gig of his into my sweaty palm. It was an odd experience listening to his version of the song when I got back to the flat. I seem to remember he'd taken out the swear-words and the band were obviously confused about how to translate our E-flat drop-tuning but to hear the voice that had been part of the very furniture of my youth singing my own words back to me of course cast an undeniable spell. More than anything though I think I perceived my early musical heroes as so much more than mere musicians. They were people who had helped me navigate my way through life, influencing my politics, suggesting how I should dress and even telling me what not to eat and so to hear such an unequivocal validation of my work by one of them was a wonderful but in some ways slightly confusing moment, like when the teacher is finally bested by his pupil, and I remember lying on my fusty purple bedspread in Moorhouse Road listening to it one drizzly afternoon overcome with a strange blend of triumph and melancholy. With hindsight relegating 'My Insatiable One' to the status of a B-side was the first in a long line of bad judgements that we made, exiling classics to the wastelands of the flip side, limiting their audience and so rendering the albums weaker by their absence but at the same time this profligacy was conscious and deliberate; we wanted every moment of our output to be notable, even, and in some ways especially the B-sides. I suppose appropriately it was very much something we had taken from The Smiths whose flip sides for a period were superlative. It made being a fan feel so thrilling, like the band were honouring your devotion with a gift, and it was this sense of breathless discovery that we wanted to continue with our work. Nonetheless if 'My Insatiable One' and 'To The Birds' and 'He's Dead' and 'The Big Time' had been on the debut it simply would have been a better record.

This was a wonderful time for Bernard and me as friends – we were tight and united and increasingly respectful of each other and of what we were at last producing together. The dank, bitter years of failure had cemented us into a hardened unit and at last it felt like the ears of the world were beginning to open to what we were doing. Our first few winters as a struggling band had been met with the usual mass shrug of indifference that greets most musical wannabes, but as we had pressed ever onwards the battle against apathy seemed if anything to become harder as we had continued to perform edgy shows to disengaged audiences that sat uncomfortably with the required default, early nineties, indie-band setting of blank, spaced-out cool. Often there had been more people on the stage than in the crowd and at one point we had played a deeply humiliating and utterly point-less gig to one single person. Finally though through a combination of bloody-mindedness, accident and evolution we had found our voice and at last people had started to listen. Bernard and I would share clove cigarettes and ride the rattling underground together, chattering excitedly, plotting and planning and bor-rowing each other's sentences and in the same way that young people know that death is inevitable but distant our own predictable disintegration as written in the annals of rock lore seemed impossibly irrelevant with just the odd flashes of discord between us pro-viding the occasional memento mori: the skull at the edge of the canvas. The overall stirring of confidence and camaraderie within the band had been growing strongly too and the change in dynamic following Justine's departure had allowed Simon especially to emerge from the fringes and reveal himself more fully to be the kind, loyal and often hilarious friend that he is, so much more than just the polite punkish cipher we first met.

We started to play small iconic London venues, always ensuring that they were dangerously oversold, heaving with steaming, sweating bodies and almost impossible to get into. This manufactured hysteria seemed in keeping with a core ethos of the band – that desire to transcend the everyday, to reach for the heightened state. I've always loved artists that seemed untouchable and otherworldly. Even a band like the Pistols despite their rags and their Highbury chants seemed cut from a different cloth to the rest of us: cartoonish and Day-Glo and somehow alien. Without wishing to come across as pompous, the whole 'we're just the same as our fans' attitude just reminds me of dads who believe themselves to be their kids' 'best friends': false, patronising and ultimately hollow. Regardless of how unfashionable a viewpoint it is, it has always struck me that any performance is essentially an elitist act and that the stage is there for a very clear purpose – to separate and elevate a band from its audience – and that the power differential therein is an essential ingredient in the drama. A gig at The Africa Centre in Covent Garden that preceded the single release was the first of these raucous, enervating little shows and I think the first time that we began to recognise that people really might want something that we possessed. I remember feeling utterly shocked by the fact that four hundred people had actually paid hard-earned money to see us. The gig itself I recall as being vaguely underwhelming as we had yet to learn to channel our nerves and feed them into our performance resulting in a slightly skittish display that lacked command and authority. By that point however it felt that the odd pratfall didn't really matter, that we were acquiring a ground-swell of goodwill that was beginning to carry us along like a friendly tide.

TOMORROW'S FISH
AND CHIP PAPER

The dissonant jarring rumble of a clutch of separate groups playing completely different songs bled through into the corridor of the Premises rehearsal rooms on Hackney Road. The place smelled of the stale sweat and cigarette butts of a thousand unsigned bands and as the kick drums thudded and the bass guitars meshed and pounded along a thin mist of dust drifted from the cracked Victorian plasterboard ceiling and settled imperceptibly on the counter of the little booth which stocked spare guitar strings and biscuits and crisps. Behind it the brusque, shuffling owner plonked two cups of milky tea on the worktop and looked at me. 'That'll be two quid,' he said. I dug into the tangled mess of my jeans pocket and fished out a few coins and gave them to him. He took the money and held my gaze. 'I saw your piece in the *Melody Maker*,' he offered with an uncharacteristic smile. 'Oh yes,' I replied brightly, half expecting to be met with a tiny nod of grudging approval. 'Best new band in Britain?' he muttered, scowling again. 'You're not even the best band in this building.'

Sometime in April that year the gathering chatter about us had provoked the weekly music paper *Melody Maker* to commission an interview to coincide with the release of the record. We'd dipped our toes into the media pond previously with a couple of insignificant new band mini-pieces but this was to be a major feature conducted by the editor Steve Sutherland who had heard the EP and felt suitably galvanised. Steve was an interesting character, obviously unnervingly bright but possessing too a steely thread of ambition and a professional journalist's rapacious pursuit of a story. In him I sensed a ruthlessly unsentimental streak and looking beyond us and into the future I think he saw in Suede not just a band but the beginnings of a movement. I had yet to acquire any real skills as an interviewee so I remember feeling slightly out of my depth and in fact Mat was more quotable, but then again he always has been.

After the interview we trundled off to one of the maze of draughty, bleak, east London photographers' studios that peppered that part of the city before the hipsters moved in. The session was with Tom Sheehan, the resident *Melody Maker* chief 'smudge', a likeable jocular Cockney who managed to get us to prance around in front of the lens in our fake-fur coats and Oxfam jackets like urchins who had found someone's dressing-up box, cajoling us into playing the part that was slowly being written for us. Even though I didn't realise it at the time I see now that so much of a photographer's skill lies in their dialogue with the subject, their ability to tease out nuances of facial expressions and attitude, hence the cliché of the *Blow-Up* David Bailey-esque stereotype lost in a parodic pantomime of desire imploring the kitten-eyed waif to 'make love to the camera'. I've never been the sort of person who can smile on cue, wondering how to do it when I see the act of smiling as a reaction rather than a response I can just willingly command, but Tom was a wily old operator and I think knew that we would want to portray ourselves as something other than the standard throng of glum-looking boys staring at their shoes which was the accepted template of the period. At the time the thought of spending an afternoon being flattered in a studio was infinitely preferable to the dole queues and dead-end jobs that we'd just left behind but with hindsight our naivety in front of the camera was unwise as I think our innocent desire to pander contributed to an early veneer of fame-hungry vacuity which we struggled with for many years. It's interesting that how one is perceived in those first skirmishes with the media is so potent, that it can continue to define you and become a rigid shell that is in some ways impossible to outgrow. There's a popular theory that famous people's emotional development is frozen at the moment they achieve fame as they begin to buffer themselves from the real world but there are parallels with the popular attitude towards them too which sometimes never matures beyond a simplistic entry point.

One Tuesday in late April Mat and I were walking along Great Marlborough Street and as we approached a newsstand I thought I saw something that looked a bit like my face on the front of *Melody Maker*. As we got closer and the image became clearer there was a weird moment of mental disconnect as I realised with a shock that the thing that appeared to be my face was exactly that and that we had been placed on the cover. Underneath our four heads and printed in bold capitals was the legend THE BEST NEW BAND IN BRITAIN, a phrase that would become inescapable for us over the next few years and one which at times we would wish we had never set eyes on. It's difficult for me to know whether the significance of this really translates to anyone brought up in an era after the dominance of the print media. The weekly music press used to be hugely relevant and influential and had the power and the reach and the circulation figures to direct and shape and mould careers. There was a strict hierarchy however, a pecking order that had to be observed, which meant that bands who were on the eve of releasing their debut single simply weren't chosen as cover stars. Having spent the wasted hours of our teenage years poring over the minutiae of their pages we knew these conventions very well so once we had recovered from the surprise we were confronted with the sheer uniqueness of our position. I think sadly many people who remember that period still see the band as a product of the press, a twisted, unholy media experiment created in the shadowy, Shelley-esque laboratories of IPC, and it was this seminal moment that provided much fuel for that particular fire; the suspicion that we were somehow complicit in the crime and guilty of that most cardinal of indie sins – inauthenticity. Of course at the time we were all far too seduced by the heady rush of something actually happening in our lives to bother caring too much about the consequences or the implications but looking back I can't help feeling that those who allowed us to be put in that situation were incredibly irresponsible and short-sighted. I simply think we weren't advised well, that those whose job it was to analyse and dissect these situations never bothered to explain that the prize that we were chasing was ultimately poisonous. We were far too in the moment to stop for even a second but it's the role of the band to be impetuous and instinctive and wild and quixotic and the role of those around them to be sober and considered and guiding. I can't help but think that we were failed on that score and were allowed to tumble headlong into the storm and that our pact with the capricious mistress of the press was ill thought-out. Hindsight is a wonderful thing though and it's easy for me to pick through these pivotal moments and criticise. I can't pretend that we weren't all desperate to succeed and in that ensuing feeding frenzy we blindly clutched at any and every means necessary. It would end up having long-reaching consequences for our career as for many we were forever cast simplistically as 'over-rated' and 'overhyped', deprecations that to this day I feel in many ways still often haunt us, a legacy of our early exaggerated profile.

This lack of sober guidance was quite revealing about the nature of our set-up and the people around us. Saul was arguably the most experienced of our mentors at the time but there was always a sense with him that he was equally, if not even more, thrilled with the commotion that was beginning to swirl around us and he would often be gripped with a maniacal, zealous energy as events began to unfold, passionately cheering on our successes very much as though they were his own, caught up in the wild journey that we found ourselves embarking on. The situation was so new that there was no rule book to consult when it came to negotiating its vicissitudes and we found our-selves unwittingly cast as the proverbial guinea-pigs in a shifting new relationship between the artist and the press that would go on to define the media landscape of the coming decade. The response to Suede was so disproportionate that there seemed to be very few historical parallels, and while it's not something that I'm particularly proud of it's something that needs to be addressed as it became an integral element to our story. For those who weren't there or who have forgotten it might give a sense of the scale of the media reaction to say that even before the debut album was released we would end up gracing *nineteen* front covers. It was a phenomenon that of course was bound to have pernicious consequences, not least with Bernard's later rejection and drift away from the band, but while the frothy delirium still seemed like fun we just gripped on to the seat in front of us and enjoyed the ride.

The EP was pencilled in for release on 11 May 1992 and once it had been recorded and mixed it was left to me to decide on the artwork. I'd always loved how album sleeves could somehow define and refract the music, how the right image could be powerful enough to become completely synonymous with the songs, and had spent endless, drifting teenage hours gazing at the work of Hipgnosis and Jamie Reid and Peter Saville. Having spent many a dreary mid-week afternoon trudging around second-hand shops and flea markets I had built up a small mildewy library of books one of which was the work of Holger Trulzsch and the model Verushka. The surreal, charged images had fascinated me for years especially one which depicted a naked girl body-painted with a man's suit and holding a gun. It seemed like a perfect expression of some of the oblique themes in the songs – the blend of threat and sexuality, the joyous confusion of androgyny – and so this became our EP artwork. The cheapened, badly made, almost Situationist quality the sleeve eventually possessed was actually a happy accident that was the result of a low budget as the record company told us that we could only afford to print a couple of colours, lending it a wonderfully childish cut-and-paste naivety – an almost homemade quality that became a visual theme in the whole series of those early record sleeves.

The reception to the release of *The Drowners* was intriguing in terms of its duality. For the vast majority of the world it passed by without a whisper of recognition making zero impact in the mainstream media and limping in at number 49 in the charts. For a small subculture however I don't think it would be disproportionate to say that it was greeted as seismic. This probably sounds horribly conceited and I'm trying to distinguish between real memories and those we manufacture after the event and to judge it all beyond my own stifling solipsism but I genuinely recall that within the world of the weekly music press and the London indie demi-monde the record achieved clamorous acclaim and even a note of infamy. I think we had unwittingly become the epicentre of converging forces, partly as raucous, rousing supplanters of the current moribund scene and partly because we had developed a panache and élan of our own – an expression of something startling and new – but mainly, I like to flatter myself, because the songs were good. I've always been a wild-eyed believer in the power of the song. I love that it's achievable with the simplest of equipment and that the keys on a piano or a typewriter simultaneously encourage and mock you with a combination of their limits and their possibilities, the secret so tantalisingly at your fingertips but still out of reach, just as when sitting down sometimes with a cheap guitar, a voice and a little inspiration you are galvanised by the sense that you could be on the threshold of unlocking something magical, of stretching yourself towards some sort of wondrous alchemy boundaried only by your own imagination. That compelling, powerful interplay between words and melody was something that had obsessed me since childhood and together with Bernard it felt like we were really beginning to speak as songwriters, something it seemed that for years had become rather a lost art.

It would be disingenuous though not to credit in all this the presence of a murky sexuality in the songs. Some of the oblique, ambiguous lines in 'The Drowners' and the shift in perspective of 'My Insatiable One' had lent the EP a charged, carnal edge which I'm sure added to the general volume of ambient chatter about the band. I was very conscious of this element of my writing, keen to tease out those threads that had always fascinated me in other people's work. I had always found most pop music so prissy and anodyne in that respect or that if sex was a subject then it was described with cartoonish vacuity and never seemed to delve beyond cliché. In an early interview I once said that I wanted to talk about 'the used condom rather than the beautiful bed' and I think that's still an accurate way to look at the thrust, ahem, of those early songs. I viewed writing about sex as I viewed writing about life: as an exploration of minutiae, delving under the layers to glance sideways at the failure and the fear, the moments of hesitation and confusion as well as the simplistic binary categories into which the subject is usually confined. Of course some would see this as trying to be deliberately titillating or controversial but at its heart it was my simple attempt to document the world I saw around me. The lens of the media would refract and reflect what I was doing back to me and I would respond to that and feed it into my subsequent writing and it would subconsciously and incrementally add thin layers to the onion of my growing persona, but no one who ushers their work into the public arena can be free from that unholy loop. At the same time though it would be duplicitous of me not to recognise that on some level I was very aware of what I was doing. What inspired me to detail sex in the songs must have been partly a desire to provoke. I've always seen it as one of the core purposes of pop music – well, good pop music anyway – to incite strong feelings, to rouse emotion and to instigate blind allegiance, and sometimes a consequence of that extremity of response is dislike and even hatred. Very early on it became obvious to me that Suede was a group that inspired passion and derision in equal measure and very little feeling towards the middle of that spectrum. It's just one of those characteristics that we have to live with for better or for worse, much like there's little someone can do about the size of their feet, so in a similar way a band has to accept what kind of band it is and work within those limits and, if they're clever, use them to their own ends.

DOGSHIT AND DIAMONDS

Simon's clattering, tribal tattoo rattled around the cavernous room and Bernard's screaming guitar played out the last few frenzied chords as 'Moving' charged towards its frantic denouement. I whipped my microphone lead in time with the pulsing, scattering rhythm and stood teetering on the monitors, staring wild-eyed into the void of the crowd, victorious and sweaty as the song crashed to its violent end. In the sudden silence that followed, the rows of bored, glum-looking students in Ned's Atomic Dustbin T-shirts shifted uncomfortably and stared at their shoes. One or two clapped half-heartedly but above the muted, smoky hubbub all over the venue the same question was being asked: 'What time are Kingmaker on?'

As the excitement had mounted following our ascent we were offered a tour support slot with a group called Kingmaker who during the early nineties had become quite popular, building up a loyal following in the medium-sized university venues of the circuit. It's never much fun playing to other people's audiences; it's hard to really penetrate beyond their sense of uncommitted curiosity and mild suspicion and generate any real energy but sometimes it's a necessary step you must take as an emerging band, gritting your teeth and steeling yourself against their muted response. I don't remember any of our performances being particularly notable for this reason but the tour was frothy and fun and we got on well with Kingmaker and I shared a few late-night beery conversations and between-sound-check chats with their singer Loz, a shy but bright and sensitive boy who I always liked. The tour's apogee was a show at the Town and Country Club in Kentish Town, just up the road from the Bull and Gate pub where we had spent many an underwhelming, unimpressive evening cutting our teeth in 1990. At the time the Town and Country was easily the biggest place we had ever played and so for that reason alone it was an occasion for us. Again I don't remember our show being anything special but it was an evening that would provoke Steve Sutherland at the *Melody Maker* to write a famously provocative review. Picking up the inkies the following Tuesday we were confronted with the headline 'PEARLS BEFORE SWINE' and the caustic phrase 'dogshit and diamonds' expressing the perceived disparity between the headliners and ourselves. Even more arch was Steve's political manipulation of the situation, using it to equate a coterie of 'dogshit' bands (Kingmaker et al) with rival publication the *NME* and associating what he saw as the 'diamond' bands (Suede et al) with the *Melody Maker*. The battle-lines were drawn and war was declared. It was an incendiary and, in a small way, a very influential piece of writing that apparently caused mass resignations when ironically Steve was appointed *NME* editor a year or so later.

Whatever your views of the merits and opinions of that particular article I don't think that you can deny its chutzpah. For me it marked the apex of inflammatory weekly music-press journalism. This was a time when picking up the papers on a Tuesday morning would mean taking your life into your hands. Reviews and comments could be savage and the invective vicious and personal and crushing and as a key figure in the eye of the storm I tasted both sides. Sometimes within the same edition I was dragged cruelly and savagely through the mud or cast equally ridiculously as some sort of demi-god. As a young man it was sometimes almost impossible to see myself as a point between these extremes as I oscillated between morbid self-reflection and vainglorious narcissism. Personally speaking I don't know how it's possible to ignore things that are being written about you and your work. Of course there are artists who claim that they 'never read their own press' and perhaps there are a few who don't but probably less than you would imagine. It's one of those musician clichés like 'we just make music for ourselves and if anyone else is interested that's a bonus', intimating blithe insouciance and a romantic suggestion that the artist is some sort of seer above such petty concerns as caring what others might think of them and more often than not it's a complete fiction. The truth is that the very act of ushering your work into the public arena is a plea for some sort of validation and response from the media; although often denigrated by a certain sort of artist many will secretly seek this, gorging on it when it is positive and writhing in discomfort when it isn't. You might assume that when press is bad you could just ignore it but I find that I need to 'work through it' in a way that almost parallels the assimilation of grief. It's difficult to know the effect it has had on me psychologically – which traits it has exaggerated and which it has suppressed – and what kind of a person I would be now without the experience. I don't think anyone escapes from that kind of distortion of truth without mental scars, but again it's part of the pact you sign when you embark on this whole merry little jaunt. Given that the rewards are so great I think what amounted to a form of abuse was seen as being acceptable – that like a modern-day gladiatorial contest the value of the prize justified its bloody pursuit. Even though people around you tell you to 'not take it personally' there's never really a moment when you can separate yourself from your persona and see the whole thing happening to someone else and as the years roll on, like dating or something, what you would assume would get easier doesn't.

Yet despite all of this, despite having been put through the wringer more times than I can remember and having been damaged on what was probably a deep, personal level by the experience, I still believe we have lost something culturally valuable now that we no longer have that kind of 'Punch and Judy' weekly music press. It probably seems easy for me to say because I wasn't on the receiving end of that particular tirade – and my point has nothing to do with the relative merits of the bands in question – but with the benefit of over twenty-five years of hindsight I think that the piece was ultimately a creative act. Sutherland knew that he was doing something more important than pissing a few people off when he wrote it. He knew he was being outrageous, unpopular, unpleasant and unnecessarily vitriolic but he also knew that his goading would ultimately inspire bands to strive to improve. He understood his role in it all and he knew the broader value of the 'press kicking', and he understood the axiomatic truth that any artist who enters into the arena of public assessment waives their right to be upset if someone doesn't like their work and that raging critiques are, in a kind of Darwinian way, part of the complex system of checks and balances that crush some bands and motivate others to go on and achieve something extraordinary. They are a disagreeable but necessary element of the ecosystem. The music press of the seventies, eighties and nineties was a charged battleground of polarisation and opinion that generated scenes. Some of these were laughable, short-lived cultural jokes but some, like punk, went on to change the world and redefine how the public saw music and in a broader sense how they saw art. When we eventually started travelling abroad we were at first viewed suspiciously by much of the foreign media, many of whom chose to see us as a product of the British music press. We would get a barrage of gruff accusations about 'the hype' and an unfair focus away from the music that we had created and were so proud of. I always thought they were kind of missing the point. For a start, hype will only take you so far. Without any substance people will soon see through its flimsy artifice and wander off towards the next shiny thing. More ironically though it seemed that the machinery of which they were so suspicious had probably been partly responsible for much of the music that they loved. Nowadays, despite a few notable exceptions, most publications seem too afraid of offending their demographic to have any worthwhile opinion, apparently supporting whatever is in their best interest regardless of its artistic worth, blandly approving of marketing campaigns and fearful of their shareholders.

This will probably get me into trouble and I'd love to be proved wrong and maybe I'm too out of touch to be able to see it clearly but unfortunately I just can't see where the game-changing scenes and the movements of the digital age are likely to come from. I feel that the defining cultural event of our times – social media – has cast such a huge shadow and even though people still passionately love music it has become more of a lifestyle accessory rather than a central, defining core of their being and because of that its impact and its generational resonance has waned. And while I'm up on my soap-box I may as well take the opportunity to blather on a little about some other broader issues. I think it should worry everyone deeply that since the decimation of the music business at first by internet piracy and then by the proliferation of streaming services it is increasingly hard for artists who make left-field marginal music to make a living. Of course there are always anomalies but I've noticed that the sort of new bands who would have had healthy lucrative careers back in the seventies and eighties and nineties making interesting, non-commercial music are struggling to survive. Clearly this raises class issues. Are we to assume that working-class voices will be virtually unheard in alternative music in a few years' time because it's just no longer seen as a viable career and the only way left-field bands can survive is if they are bank-rolled by well-off parents? However there are wider and even more troubling implications beyond this. Right now it's a phenomenon that probably doesn't unduly worry those denizens of the upper echelons of the music industry who are still earning big money making mainstream pop music but it really should. The strata of the creative world are all linked and in many ways co-dependent rather like an ecosystem. Not wishing to sound over-simplistic it seems to me that the more creative marginal musicians have always been the creatures that the commercial artists have fed off, diluting and sanitising and popularising their ideas. In the same way that if plant life were to die out it would create a chain of events that would lead to the extinction of carnivores, so I believe that the work done at the margins of the music industry is utterly essential to the health of the music world as a whole. Without this motor that generates ideas we can envisage a sort of bleak cultural vacuum whereby the only starting points that commercial artists have are increasingly based on copies of previous historic successes leading to a horribly nostalgic, ersatz musical landscape that is meaningless and devoid of any traction or worth or vitality. Some might argue that we arrived at that point many years ago; the success of *The X Factor* and *Faux-town* amongst other pop movements would seem to support their case and mainstream music has always had a proclivity towards sentimentalism, but at least there are glimmers of interesting work still appearing. It worries me though that taken to its logical point we will be seeing more than just a dearth of ideas and possibly the beginnings of an end game.

Back to my little story however. Years later when I reconnected with Justine I would get to know Loz quite well as he lived in a room in her house in Notting Hill. By that time his band had disintegrated along with his ambitions of success and he was living life at a drifting, melancholy pace. He was always a gentle soul but I fear he had had something thrust upon him he wasn't ready for and so fell prey to the savage jaws of the music machine, damaged by the same wheels that create success in some and grind others into the dirt. The thin line between success and failure in bands has always fascinated me – the mechanics that dictate that some will go on to become a world-beating phenomenon while others will politely pale away into an elephants' graveyard of cultural insignificance. Obviously raw talent and hard work and resilience play huge roles in these outcomes but beyond that it does often seem, even from an insiders' point of view, almost a random process. I think everyone has listened to a band sometimes and wondered how on earth they became successful and I'm sure there are swathes of people who feel exactly this with regard to Suede.

Often I think there is just an element of their character that resonates with a whole tribe of people. This can be an unusual or exciting way of doing things, a musical gimmick, an unpredictability or an attitude or even just the fickle hand of fate. I've always had an idealistic and probably woefully naive belief that it is the quality of your work that will steer you towards success but when I see a band like Echo and the Bunnymen for example propping up festival bills and playing support slots to paltry, disinterested audiences after having made some of the most celestial, life-affirming music of the eighties while some of their contemporaries fill the arenas of the world I have to admit that the whole process is beyond any sort of formula and obviously reflects the absolute subjectivity of music and art in general. Sadly for Loz his band would join the legions of the unsung, the indifferent machine spitting him out on to the pile while others around him continued their giddying ascent.

EFFETE SOUTHERN WANKERS

The four of us stood on the tiny smoky back-room stage of the Gourock Bay Hotel as the final guitar phrase of 'Pantomime Horse' coiled slowly to an end. Our eyes were cast to the floor, our faces shadowed by the wash of red coming from the single-gelled flood-light fixed to a baton in the ceiling. The paltry scattered crowd glowered at us balefully through a light smatter-ing of dutiful applause and as the sound of shuffling feet on the sticky floor filled the room the last few sol-itary claps died away and there was a stark moment of sullen silence as we looked at the handwritten set lists and readied ourselves for the next song. Suddenly from somewhere out of the shadows, loud and clear against the tense hush a gruff Glaswegian voice bellowed out, *'You effete Southern wankers!'*

As the tyres of the off-white Ford Transit span against

the dark rubberised asphalt of the M8 we sped past slip roads and fly-overs eating up the broken white lines, patchy scrub-land verges and sober, monolithic road signs disappearing in our rear-view mirror. Charlie sat up front clutching the wheel, speeding us ever onwards while the rest of us in the back of the lightless van lolled and floundered on the mattress, rolling in acquiescence as the vehicle gently listed against the buffeting wind. And so, lost to a drifting, strip-lit world of motorway service-station breakfasts and fraught sound checks and a hinterland of cheap, vinegary wine and dressing-room cheese platters, the 1992 *Drowners* tour rumbled on. Endless afternoons were spent fiddling with sticks of celery and cling film backstage in low-level venues while we waited as the scant crew set up and our evenings were lost in the throes of charged performance and crazed Dionysian excess; the days and nights a strange dissonant blend of the mundane and the extraordinary. Our ephemeral deification by the music press provoked mixed reactions around the country. The hostile, stony-faced audience to whom we played in Gourock was obviously suspicious of what it probably saw as a group of pampered, privileged, metropolitan-elite press darlings. If the situation hadn't felt so genuinely intimidating I would have collapsed laughing at the brilliant absurdity of the insult that had been hurled at us: a genius blend of eloquence, invective and irony. The other memory I have from that show was of Mat emerging from the urinals after the gig and telling us he'd just been asked threateningly by some swaying, hulking thug whether he'd 'fuckin' seen where Suede have gone?' and been forced to affect his bad version of a Scots accent for some sort of muffled, uncommitted reply – a bit like Withnail when confronted in the toilets by a bellicose Irishman in one of the film's many famous scenes. Not all the little regional shows during this period had that kind of truculent tone however. One of my fondest memories was playing the Southampton Joiners Arms where it seemed like something quite wonderful was happening. Despite the modest surroundings, the shabby flock-wallpapered room and the stacks of plastic pint glasses, as I looked out over the small sea of faces it felt like a 'moment', like everyone there knew something special was happening and that it was beyond anyone's control. If I had one personal memory that seems to define the point when Suede really 'happened' it would actually be that show. I remember a surge of euphoria as for the first time I felt that the band and the audience were united towards the same ends; that crazed, unstoppable rush of power that you sometimes get as a performer when you realise that there's almost nothing that you can do wrong – a kind of dizzying illusion of perfection created by a willing conspiracy between us and the crowd and the right conditions. It was the first time that I was really aware of that flow of energy, the first time it had dawned on me that playing live was about so much more than just dutifully presenting your songs and that the difference between a good gig and a great gig was the complicity of the punters and the loop of response and counter-response between them and those on the stage. Occasionally it can feel like an audience doesn't understand that it has a role too, that unlike attending the cinema the manner in which we play is hugely influenced by its reaction. Over the years it's something that has quietly obsessed me as it becomes increasingly clearer that Suede, possibly more than most bands, needs that feedback for it to work and sometimes making the evening successful means striving to manufacture that.

Another special memory I have from the gigs around this time is of one at a little pub in Belfast. The show was spirited, but it wasn't until an odd moment of serendipity when Bernard's guitar cut out and the song broke down halfway through only to be rescued by the mass singing of the crowd all crooning along to the chorus that it really took off. There was something so humbling and lovely about it, a glorious sense of unity that made us all break out into huge, shit-eating grins; one of those extraordinary and unpredictable moments that sparks and lights the touch paper. The rest of the show descended into a wonderfully sticky sort of riot and finally after it had juddered to its deaf-ening denouement we made our shaky, sweaty way back to the Europa Hotel, which incidentally we had been almost proudly informed was the most frequently bombed hotel in Europe. I remember all of us gathering in the bar and while we were chatting and sipping at our bottles of Beck's suddenly becoming aware of a ragged, lurching choir of voices outside. After a few moments we realised that they were singing 'The Drowners' and that half the audience had followed us to the hotel to serenade us from the street. It was both a heartwarming and hilarious moment as beaming and giggling we gathered on the balcony and waved mock-pompously like the Windsors after a Royal Wedding while the little crowd cheered and the evening traffic bustled by. Slowly then we became aware that a small but passionate throng of devotees was beginning to follow us around – a tight little knot of fans from places like Tring and Lyme Regis and Hebden Bridge who would turn up at the sound checks and with whom we would sit and chat after the shows, huddled in the stuffy, littered dressing rooms smoking Benson and Hedges and juggling oranges and chattering wildly about music until the small hours when we would stagger back into the Transit and make our way blearily home to London or to collapse in the twin rooms of some cheap local bed and breakfast. This was back when everything still felt wonderfully guileless, before any sort of band/fan divide had been established, when we were all still genuinely grateful and slightly surprised that people had invested their time and money to come and see us. Of course all four of us had been fans ourselves and so to see others similarly inspired felt somehow strangely satisfying, like we were passing on a baton or closing a circle, or repaying some sort of cosmic debt, and even though our egos were obviously burgeoning due to the attention this was still at a stage when it was all small-scale enough for us to see this wonderful carnival of people that we were encountering as new friends. We loved meeting these wild-eyed boys and girls and would sit there in the smoky backstage areas signing T-shirts and jabbering excitedly about music as the raucousness grew and the cans scattered and the ash-trays heaved. Touring was so novel to us that the whole day would somehow merge – the gigs themselves and the parties afterwards and even the dead hours spent travelling and eating service-station sandwiches all melding into the same joyful experience. Over the years as we became more professional with our approach we would learn to delineate these things, ring-fencing our performances and separating them from the chaos that surrounded us to deal with the hard grind of touring, and I think sadly we ended up losing something precious, but those early playful hours spent hanging out with that growing throng of lovely people were special and in many ways essential to the nature of the band we would become. It was the beginnings of the loyal and passionate Suede community that I am happy to say still mills around us today, an assemblage of wonderful zealots who never cease to amaze me with their stamina and their loyalty and their dedication.

During those lovely, fizzy summer days of 1992 it felt like our lives were at a tipping point. As we lay on the grass together outside the sound check at the Windsor Old Trout chewing on our salad kebabs and staring up at the rippling sky I remember feeling a tingle of affection for everyone, a strange fusing of calm and impatient anticipation, a thrilling sense of purpose made sweeter by the periods of frustration and stasis and a strong urge of wanting to pry prematurely into the next chapter. It was during those shows that it felt like a real hysteria was building and during one of my many forays into the bosom of the front row one evening a couple of fans grabbed tightly to my shirt and in the good-humoured tussle ended up ripping it so that I emerged from the mosh pit tattered and ragged and barely clothed. It was a beautiful, spontaneous moment that started to become a bit of a ritual at our gigs. Before it became predictable I secretly enjoyed this joyous, tactile ceremony, and so night after night I would be grabbed and semi-willingly stripped and forced the next day to go out and buy something to replace the lost garment. It seemed easiest to buy some cheap bit of tat that I wouldn't mind being shredded so after the sound checks I would trawl the local junk shops and buy crappy old nylon shirts and flimsy blouses – ridiculous chiffony second-hand clothes whose only purpose was to last the first few songs. It fleetingly became a style and many of the photographers who were beginning to swarm around us focused on it as a deliberate 'look' and I suppose it was but in a less preconceived way than it might have appeared. I would be lying if I pretended that I wasn't aware of a sexual thread to the persona that was beginning to be woven around me. It sounds faintly comical to me now sitting here writing as a middle-aged, married father but I did definitely toy with themes of androgyny, playing on those confusing margins of interpretation to which we are all sometimes open. Again, my adoption of any 'femininity' in my style was partly a twisted, misjudged expression of grief but also an assimilation of the image of myself that was being projected back to me by the media. At some point in that year I did an interview with a long-forgotten alternative music mag called *Lime Lizard* in which I talked about how when songwriting I had inhabited personas like housewives and gay men and switched from the first person to the third in order to shift perspectives and keep the writing fresh for myself. To make a point I blithely mentioned that during these moments I viewed myself as a kind of 'bisexual man who's never had a homosexual experience'. It was to become one of the stupidest and most over-quoted things I have ever said and will probably appear on my gravestone. I deeply regret the naivety of the young man who said it not because he was lying or fictionalising at all but because he failed to realise that there is zero space for subtlety and shades of meaning in the modern media when it comes to salacious subjects. If you speak to large groups of people through the press you have to use quite simplistic terms or your intended meaning will be smothered in a tide of misinterpretation, hence the proliferation of so many uninspired dullards blathering on about how they are going to 'save rock and roll' or possibly how they are going to 'destroy rock and roll' etc. etc. Of course the famous quote resonated with the idea of me that was circulating and maybe I'm being disingenuous in suggesting that I wasn't aware of that and that I didn't use it to my own ends but I can't help hating that for some people it placed me neatly in a box labelled 'bisexual' when in fact I was trying to express in my desire not to be categorised something of the exact opposite. If anything interested me about the broader subject of androgyny and the margins of sexuality it was Nietzschean ideas about art combining the masculine and feminine which was something that had been introduced to me via the work of the artist Allen Jones and his *Hermaphrodite* series; a brave and intriguing expression of his integration of the male and female elements of his nature. It wasn't intended as crass sexual tourism or a dreary homage to seventies glam rock or certainly not as any witless attempt to be controversial. To be honest I think it was a mark of the essentially laddish, conservative nature of the alternative music industry back then that it was given any airtime and seen as in any way shocking or provocative. A bit like Coco Chanel's famous utterance about there being no ugly women, only lazy ones, it was one of those kind of quotes that registered powerfully with how the public were beginning to see me and playing within those narrow boundaries of definition it became all the more impossible to shrug off. Within the band it became looming and ubiquitous and for a while inescapable and then eventually amusing and finally just boring. Sometimes the only way to deal with things is to deflect them with humour so as it took on a kind of life of its own we began to refer to it as the 'bicycle that's never had a puncture' quote. Well, it seemed funny at the time.

When I cast my mind back to those days and to the person that I was I'm certain that there was another layer of motivation tied up within the whole thing. Strangely I think that I was trying to articulate that I was an emotional being rather than a sexual one. I realise that it sounds like a contradiction but it was on some level an innocent attempt to almost neutralise my sexuality, to blur the lines and to dispense with gender boundaries and present my work as primarily that of a person rather than that of a man or a woman or a straight person or a gay person or even a bisexual person. Certainly the more reflective pieces like 'The Next Life' or 'Sleeping Pills' or 'Pantomime Horse' were intended to be – to steal a phrase from the modern vernacular – 'gender neutral'. It feels though that the more I try to explain my motivations the more disingenuous I sound and the deeper a hole I dig for myself. However you look at it my aspirations were at best naive and at worst clunky – a failure to understand the media and its lack of nuance.

THE ONLY THING WORSE
THAN BEING TALKED ABOUT
IS NOT BEING TALKED ABOUT

The music throbbed around the smoky back room of the pub and I pushed my way to the bar, wriggling between the press of bodies, the rubber soles of my shoes sticky against the stale spilt beer that had dried on the ash-laden floor. I gestured hopefully towards the barman and held out my crumpled five-pound note and noticed a girl darting sideways glances my way from the other end of the counter, her eyebrows arched quizzically, her chin raised slightly in a gesture of mild defiance and the hint of a smile flickering across her pretty face. As I paid for my drink and the throng between us cleared slightly I realised that she had sidled up to me. I turned to meet her stare and as I looked into her pale blue eyes she spoke at last. 'You're the singer from Suede, aren't you?' 'Yes,' I replied smugly, my gaze wandering over the light spray of freckles that dusted the skin around her cheekbones, my mind already imagining what her mouth might feel like pressed against mine. 'I thought you were,' she answered. 'I think your band are shit.'

A group must always be writing, always be recording or always be touring. These are their only acceptable states of being and they comprise the Holy Trinity of its self-definition. It's the way in which, shark-like, it swims ever forward, always moving, always in a state of stealth and readiness and industry. And so in quiet acquiescence to this principle our next single was scheduled to be 'Metal Mickey' and flushed with the illusion of success and armed with plectrums and Dictaphones we were packed off to Protocol Studios with Ed Buller again as producer. This time however we were to learn that a formulaic approach doesn't always work. The first version we recorded of the song was I think an attempt to follow the template of 'The Drowners'. It was light, it was poppy, it was bitterly disappointing. For some reason either Ed or Bernard had decided to layer the main rhythm guitar with a series of overdubs which made the whole thing sound like Status Quo, utterly alien to the spirit of the raw, primal, almost lascivious throb of the live version. Sometimes when making music there is an inverse law for the relationship between the power of the part and the number of things playing it. Sometimes what has become known as the 'Phil Spector' approach to creating size through repeated overdubs just results in a weak, underwhelming mesh of sounds. Sometimes less really is more.

Listening to the mix through the NS-10s on one of those ubiquitous, black-leather, studio control-room sofas was the first time that I'd felt the old sour disappointment in what we were doing for a long while. In a rare moment of clarity and honesty we realised that what we had produced simply wasn't good enough. We reconvened at Maison Rouge Studios in Fulham and approached the whole thing differently, choosing to record it in a style that was much more akin to the simpler, grittier way we had been it playing on stage. With hindsight I think if anything we should have followed that instinct even further. Secretly I was slightly nervous that the single wasn't as good as 'The Drowners' and that the recorded version never really matched the live version in terms of visceral energy. I don't think it was helped by the somewhat self-conscious key change at the end, which still makes me wince a little. It made it all sound a bit 'Mickey Most', taking the track into a safe retro-pop territory rather than the brutish sonic threat that it should have been but overall we pretended we were happy with the results and let the tide of events buoy us along. For me however the highlight of the record was the B-side

'He's Dead', a relatively overlooked gem in the Suede canon of overlooked gems.

At some point Bernard had written a piece of music that he called 'Dixon' as the wobbling, wandering guitar part reminded him of the theme tune to an old TV show called *Dixon of Dock Green*. Try as I might I simply couldn't find the right melody and lyric to turn it into a song. The band would run through it in rehearsal, thrilling to its churning momentum while I sat sulking in the corner, mute and impotent and frustrated with myself. Bernard became increasingly irritated that I couldn't respond, knowing that there was potentially a great song in there somewhere if I could just find the right parts to unlock it. The record company had hired me a little writing room in Nomis Studios in Olympia so I could spend the idle hours of my days off hunched over my four-track portastudio drinking stewed tea and warbling half-ideas into my microphone. One day I shuffled down there on the number 28 bus and started to work yet again on the track. I'd been out somewhere the night before and during a clamorous, drunken conversation at the back of a noisy venue had misheard someone saying what sounded like the words 'animal nitrate'. Loving the playful blend of childishness and dark suggestion I had scurried off to the toilets and under the flickering fluorescent lights I had scribbled the phrase down in one of the many notebooks I used to keep in my pockets before the invention of the iPhone, and then forgot all about it until the next day when I opened my book and saw it staring back at me. Sometimes a title can be enough to unlock a song and suggest a theme which as a writer you just need to follow, stumbling blindly after it like Theseus following Ariadne's thread. I saw in it a louring landscape of sink estates and broken homes and twisted, sexual power play, and when married to the music I thrilled to its strange blend of murky insinuation and gnarled pop hooks. I'd always had a desire to pollute the mainstream with something poisonous, something that it doesn't realise is harmful until it's too late and saw in 'Animal Nitrate' the perfect vehicle for that. The song would become in many ways if not our most successful then possibly our most defining moment, the lyrics allowing it to become a kind of manifesto of intent, an unofficial national anthem for the land of Suede.

During the autumn of 1992 'Metal Mickey' was released and we marched relentlessly onwards through our tour of the toilets of Great Britain with ripped shirts and tinnitus playing bonkers, sweaty London shows at iconic, rammed little venues like the 100 Club on Oxford Street and the SW1 in Victoria. The single had gone top twenty and so we had predictably pranced like puppets around the studios of *Top of the Pops* and appeared on the cover of the *NME* and tilted with an unfamiliar breed: the mainstream media who as yet didn't seem to know what to make of us and were probably expecting not to have to care. Within a year we would be parodied on TV by *Spitting Image* and by David Baddiel and by Matt Lucas. Appearing on *Top of the Pops* was for bands of our era one of those hugely memorable career milestones. Like most people of my age I had whiled away many a rainy Thursday evening after school gazing at its glitzy parade of hair-dos and hysteria and so being invited to play ourselves felt like we had penetrated some hushed and privi-leged inner sanctum. The reality of course, like most of these things, was very different as we were herded into a bleak little dressing room in Boreham Wood one morning and made to wait for hours, hunched over cold cups of tea and a plate of biscuits while var-ious chart poppets minced around perfecting their dance routines during camera rehearsals. My abiding memory of the experience wasn't so much the gestural pantomime of the performance but instead the amus-ing lunch that we ate in a canteen that was shared by the *EastEnders* cast and crew, all of us suppressing giggles as we sat at a table chewing on our baked pota-toes next to Arthur Fowler. Despite the odd moment of bathos it definitely felt like we had moved up to the next stage but this, I think, was the point when the cracks started to appear. Throughout this early period when the press started to snap around our heels it seemed that one issue was obsessing them all: how we were dealing with 'the pressure'. There has always been a kind of stubbornness in Suede, a sense that we simply won't give people what they want if we feel it's just on their terms and so we would deflect the question with a carefree nonchalance muttering stock answers like 'the only pressure is the one we feel from ourselves' or something similarly formulaic. Looking back though the reality was very different and like water finding its way through the cracks it began to seep its way into our world in ways that I didn't expect. I remember a period around this time when before gigs I would childishly develop phantom 'illnesses', sitting there in the dressing rooms coughing and spluttering like a caricature of a consumptive poet only to emerge minutes before show-time when the adrenaline kicked in to prance nimbly on to the stage. The rest of the band seemed fairly unopinionated on the matter – they probably thought I was attention-seeking – but maybe they realised it was part of my complex self-defence mechanism that helped me deal with the smothering weight of expectation that was being placed upon us to which deep down I desperately wanted to respond, using it as a kind of built-in excuse should I fail to perform.

The sheer pace of life alone at this point was becoming enervating: my days were backed up with endless interviews and the dressing rooms were a constant procession of make-up artists and French journalists and big-shot American A&R men who wanted to come backstage and 'touch base'. At first of course the surreal novelty of this mad carnival was great fun; we kept them all at arm's-length and gave them unflattering nicknames and did silly impressions but after a while it began to feel that we were being dragged along from holding pen to holding pen like livestock. It's remarkable how literally anything, no matter how seemingly beguiling, can become everyday and even unpleasant but I've always hated it when pop stars moan about their lives – it seems like a brattish, churlish and ultimately patronising response to what is of course a charmed life, an unrealistic position of fortune and privilege. Our continued exposure to the media and the vague whiff of notoriety that was wafting around us was making me if not 'famous' then certainly recognisable. I often still reflect on the strange levels of celebrity to which I have been exposed as they seem to say something pertinent about the band itself. I think it's almost impossible for anyone in the public eye to really know exactly how famous or otherwise they really are. It's one of those unquantifiable things that is made even more impossible to gauge because the experience itself skews your judgement. Over time the band has slowly drifted into a position very much left of the mainstream so thankfully these days I'm perfectly able to walk down busy streets and only occasionally get the odd intense stare but there was a point in 1993 when something as simple as that was almost impossible. There seems to be a peculiar duality in people's response to me. Generally these days it is characterised by indifference, but occasionally it will provoke gushing, emotional encounters which hopefully I have acquired the know-how to negotiate politely. Well, most of the time anyway. At first when the experience is still a novelty it feels refreshing and amusing. The very act of jumping up on to a stage and playing music is an act of vanity. It's saying: 'Look at me, aren't I great!' so 'fame' is just a natural extrapolation of that first innocent venture. Again artists who have a sort of 'I never wanted to be famous, I'm just a simple musician' attitude I think are misunderstanding an instinct at the very centre of themselves and being disingenuous to the point of duplicity. If that were so then why bother ever stepping outside your bedroom? What they actually mean is: 'I secretly wanted to be famous but only exactly on my terms and for the consequences of my fame and success not to have any bad sides'. Unfortunately it doesn't work like that. Success, fame, whatever you want to call it, is a prickly mistress: unpredictable, mercurial, disloyal and ultimately poisonous. Like some wicked fairy-tale queen she is alluring and veiled and tantalising at first but soon reveals a venomous, malignant core when the clothes are strewn. Surely we all know this – it's woven into the fabric of contemporary folklore and it's one of those axiomatic truths that litter the landscape of talk shows and magazine articles and TV dramas. It's part of the great karmic law which states that for every up there is a down. We might all know it deep inside but acting on that knowledge is a different matter. My own dalliance with her resulted in my becoming a baseball-capped caricature of paranoia as I predictably descended into collapse and personal disintegration and addiction, but you'll have to wait to hear about that jolly little episode.

STYLE IS THE ART
OF OMISSION

On those dark, drizzly winter mornings when I was first pondering the idea of writing this book I was constantly wrestling with the question of whether I would be able to describe what is an essentially somewhat graceless struggle with any poetry or charm especially when, to be frank, the poetry and charm in your life seem to ebb away with the more success you achieve – 'the richer we are, the poorer we become' to misquote Martin Luther King. In many ways in order to succeed you have to sacrifice a tiny bit of yourself. I suppose it's that famous 'pact with the devil' trope and although the image might be melodramatic I think that it contains a grain of truth. When I can be bothered to reflect on the person that I was in the early years of my life he seems very different from the one that I was slowly becoming as the band began their eventual ascent.

Although I'm trying to not be unnecessarily nostalgic there are always things that you can learn about yourself from yourself and sometimes it's important to reflect on the callow, diffident boy that was once me and wonder how much of him is still there. As we fought our way through, scrabbling and scrambling up the long, hard slope I willingly surrendered part of myself and my view of the world became increasingly myopic and specialist, narrowing down to the cramped limits of the London indie demi-monde, no longer able to drift and wallow, an ambitious steeliness supplanting any winsome innocence. At this moment I think it's important to mention how all-consuming being in a band is. There is absolutely no such thing as being able to do it part-time. Even in the nascent stages when you are clambering up the slippery pole your life takes on an incredibly monotheistic hue shrinking to a chase to reach the check-points on your list of career milestones. When you're not working on it you're talking about it and when you're not talking about it you're thinking about it. Even when you're asleep you're dreaming about it. Sometimes when life accelerates the only way to survive the raw speed is to step away and catch your breath. Bands who forget the reasons why they first became a band are those that are destined to crash and burn but during those first dizzy days of early success it can be so hard to remember that as you stumble like a tottering toddler from shiny bauble to shiny bauble.

The simple joys of creating music together become supplanted by different, less wholesome ambitions as you learn to become someone else – someone you end up liking less.

During those sober snatched moments away from the tyranny of touring and the bizarre cavalcade that was starting to swirl around us we retreated to the shelter of doing what we really loved – working on the songs that would make up the rest of the debut album. Like most debuts, it would be mainly comprised of live favourites but as we had recklessly discarded three or four great pieces as B-sides we needed more material. This was the kind of arena where Bernard was at his best – he instilled in all of us a zealous drive, a restless, puritanical sense that unless we were creating new work then we were essentially worthless. It's an ethos that has been part of the band from those very early days and if we have any vitality and relevance today it's very much thanks to that and, yes, very much thanks to him. One day I drifted over to his flat in West Hampstead and we made tea and chatted and he picked up his red 335 and started playing a winding arpeggio piece he'd written that was punctuated by delicate trills and melted into a stormy, stirring chorus. I started singing a falsetto line over the verse and hurriedly went about recording it on one of the many Dictaphones into which I would warble squeaky half-ideas much to the band's general piss-taking. The song eventually became 'She's Not Dead' and the lyric I wrote to it was a vignette about the death in the early eighties of my Auntie Jean. That sober autumn afternoon however listening to the click of the radiators and watching the leaves scatter outside the window as Bernard played has always stayed in my head as a wonderful, misty, probably sentimental memory somehow symbolising an often overlooked unity that we enjoyed a lot in the early days. I remember the feeling of respect as we worked together, a sense of mutual purpose and the notion that something special was again magically at our fingertips. On my birthday that year I'd been predictably up all night partying at Moorhouse Road with Alan and the kind of random group of odd people who at the time seemed to always gravitate towards us. After they had all eventually staggered off home Alan and I had collapsed on to the tatty sofa, smoking and listening to music when suddenly there was a knock at the door and Bernard and Saul were on the doorstep bearing gifts. I probably wasn't making much sense by that point but I ushered them upstairs and offered them tea and they sat and chatted as I stood there swaying and trying to focus my eyes. Around that time I had bought myself a cheap old upright piano and taken off the front panel to expose the machinery to give it a kind of pre-war pianola effect. After a while Bernard sat at it and began to play a beautiful, delicate, lilting waltz-time piece that he'd written. There was something so special about the way he played it – naive and charming and somehow circumspect – like he was still courting the instrument. It had a marvellous unlearned quality that seemed to almost lend it the feel of a child's piano exercise. Later he told me that it was inspired by Beethoven's 'Moonlight' Sonata and once I had sobered up I started writing the words that became the song 'The Next Life'. For a while now, influenced by the understated finale of Neil Young's *After The Gold Rush*, we had been talking about ending the album with a smaller, more intimate track, something that stepped away from the rock guitar format and left the listener able to catch their breath. In this new song we thought we had at last found it.

The album sessions had started at Angel Studios in Islington earlier that year but it wasn't until we got to Master Rock Studios just off Kilburn High Road that it felt like the record was starting to come together. I have wonderful memories of those days: the heady sense of anticipation as I jumped on to the 31 bus from Chepstow Road with sharpened pencils in my pockets and holes in my shoes and little things like the novelty of there actually being soap in the toilet when I got there and sitting in the control room as endless cups of tea cooled and the winding, labyrinthine guitar intro to 'Pantomime Horse' curled like smoke in the air. It was an exciting time to be in Suede. There was a genuine sense among us that despite there being nothing approaching a scene yet we were at the cusp of an event that was more than just another band making another album. Of course looking at the debut in a historical context it's easy to see now how it led on to a guitar music movement during that decade but I honestly remember while we were working on it there being a frisson, a strange almost deranged zeal, a feeling that what we were doing was worthwhile and bigger than us and our petty little private dramas. Personally I also remember feeling like I had been snatched wonderfully away from something unpleasant, like one of those lucky, rescued boys in a Dickens novel: Oliver Twist waking up at Mr Brownlow's house with the sunlight streaming in through the windows, the memory of Bill Sykes just a distant shadow. I think all of us felt somehow grateful, to what or whom I don't know but as we chipped away at the record we did so with the flicker of a smile playing across our faces and a breathless sense of purpose.

There were still a couple of gaps though; one piece that had a working title of 'Stonesy' due to its simple, bluesy feel was proving particularly elusive to me but in the same way that 'Animal Nitrate' had taken some time to get right we were all convinced it was worth the pursuit. I'd met an artist, a volatile, tempestuous young woman with whom I was conducting a frenetic, exhausting and often fiery relationship. We had just been to Paris together and had returned to the twenty-four-hour party that was life in Moorhouse Road to be confronted with the sharp end of Alan's ruthless hedonism. Inevitably we all overdid it and in the death throes of the evening she had ended up fainting and tumbling on to the floor like a sack of potatoes. In those desperate, breathless few moments of panic and fear as we tried to revive her the jagged edge of our heedless lives seemed to be revealed to us and as the sweat beaded on my forehead I felt starkly confronted by the fragility of existence itself. The artist thankfully recovered but the episode left a deep chill in me and a few days later I would use the experience and weld it into what became 'So Young' – a song about hedonism and mortality and hope and the devil-may-care abandon of youth. Once my vocal was recorded we all stepped back to assess it. It was missing something to act as an antidote to the simple rocky core so Ed stepped in and delivered a beautiful, lyrical piano part, which I suppose if I'm honest was a little in debt to Mike Garson's untethered, wandering solo on 'Aladdin Sane'. In fact, when I met the unnervingly charming writer of that song for a piece organised by the *NME* around that time I excitedly played it to him, introducing it with the words 'there's quite a lot of you in this one'. Ed is the son of a composer and a cultured keyboard player in his own right and rock scholars will know that he used to play with The Psychedelic Furs back in the eighties. His part brought out a real poetry in the music that the track had been missing and in our excitement we earmarked it as the opener on the album. During my vocal take I had been shrieking unintelligible words before the main body of the song to create a kind of unruly atmosphere of anticipation, a sense of rowdy excitement. The more I thought about it the more I liked the bloody-minded idea of leaving them in the mix. It appealed to me that what was looking like possibly becoming a hugely talked-about record would start with words that no one could understand. I pictured scribbling, rewinding journalists scratching their heads and hunching over their speakers and chuckled to myself.

To be frank I don't think the debut was as strong as it could have been. It would have been a better record if we had had the long-term vision to replace light-weight fillers like 'Animal Lover' with virtually any of the recent B-sides and with the wonder of hindsight I find it sonically a little thin and over-dubbed and missing some of the thump and raw edge of the live versions. The phenomenon known jokingly as 'coke ear' was probably partly to blame for the record's lack of bass heft but nonetheless I think Ed saw in us a band that could transcend the usual boundaries of the rock format and potentially mirror his own more ambitious visions. With songs like 'Sleeping Pills' and 'So Young' this approach worked but more indelicate tracks like 'Moving' were ruined by naive attempts at studio trickery and basic misunderstandings of their merits and strengths. I don't mean for this to come across as disparaging towards Ed because we certainly weren't forced into these production decisions but I suppose when you review your life's work it's important to be honest about how you see it, perceived successes meaning nothing without the recognition of failure. The album has a feel though which I still love: it rages and it screams, it yelps and it whispers and in a strange sort of way captures some truth of who we were at that moment in our lives – youthful, impertinent, ambitious and flawed. In my more self-important moments I sometimes allow myself to see it as a record that held up a cracked mirror to John Major's Britain, capturing something of its dreariness and reflecting an image of a broken, indifferent world and a sense of what it was like to be poor and marginal and powerless within it.

When looking back it's tempting to wonder what might have been and I often think that the choice of the next single can be seen as an interesting 'sliding doors' moment in Suede's career. Originally Bernard and I especially had been desperate to release 'Sleeping Pills', seeing in it something of the depth of our ambition, the sweep and the scale that we wanted to eventually head towards. As soon as the ragged terrace chant of 'Animal Nitrate' was written however and it became a kind of sonic juggernaut those plans changed. Saul sidled up to me purposefully one day by the pool table in Master Rock and laid out his case. From a record company perspective and in a short-term sense it was obviously the right thing to do; the song was dark yet anthemic, troubling yet catchy and in terms of its chart performance and accrued radio play releasing it was absolutely the right decision. I can't help but speculate on how the future would have unfolded if the other more delicate side of our work had been exposed to the public instead. Suede has always both suffered and benefited from a polarity at its core. As writers we have always been able to oscillate between simple pop hooks and widescreen landscapes and in a way even though it has made us what we are I think it's something that has confused people whose attention has never wandered beyond our fringes. What I mean is that there were two routes the band could have taken and I think we took the most obvious one. Whether the other route would have been better for us no one will ever really know but it's something I often quietly ponder. It's fascinating how decisions like these although not actually art themselves have a kind of creativity of their own. In the same way that in journalism an editor's choices of inclusion or omission can change the message of a piece, so a record company's actions can have a hugely creative element, shaping and defining the very essence of what a band is perceived to be.

As the snowball of anticipation grew the New Year greeted us with an invitation from the Brits to play at their forthcoming event in February. It seemed to coincide in a timely way with the scheduled release of 'Animal Nitrate' and so as we were still ravenous for success and exposure and had yet to understand the maxim of style being the art of omission we accepted. I've never liked the Brits and I never will and I think the feeling is mutual. It seems to reward sales over art, scale over content: a glitzy parade of shallow facades and bottomless egos, a room full of overfed men and overdressed women making underwhelming conversation. We stumbled unwashed into the party with faded second-hand clothes and badly dyed hair and went about conducting an unruly insurrection of a performance, throwing down our instruments at the end and storming off in a kind of frothy, arrogant tantrum. The sea of shocked faces that stared back at us was just grist to the mill. We felt so wonderfully out of place, revelling in the glorious incongruity: the flies in the ointment, the worms in the apple. The whole thing felt laughably silly at the time but now looking back it has a genuine air of danger, like it captured something important concerning our eternally uncomfortable relationship with the music industry itself.

BREAKFAST AT HEATHROW

The fusty, rattling carriage of the Piccadilly Line tube train slowly heaved into the station at Heathrow Terminal 3, the spectral reflection of my wan, candle-coloured skin replaced by the flickering sodium strip-lighting of the artificially illuminated platform and the familiar, iconic heraldry of the London Underground logo. My fingers brushed against the coarse pelt of the nylon seat cover as I located my blue plastic shopping bag. This was my 'luggage' for my first ever trip to America and contained nothing much more than some clean underwear, a dog-eared copy of *The Diary of a Drug Fiend*, my notebooks and a cheese and pickle sandwich I had made for the flight. As I was always running late I hadn't had time to wash my hair and so had covered it in Batiste dry shampoo, all patchy and cobwebby against my badly done home-dye job making me look like a cross between Edward

Scissorhands and Miss Havisham. Even though we were being chased by every major record company in the world I still hadn't enough money to buy myself any proper shoes and so my socks were wet where the holes in the soles had let through the rainwater that had pooled in puddles on the pavements on that damp summer day. I don't think I was in any particular hurry as I ambled towards the airline desk where we had all arranged to meet but when I realised that I was the only one there I casually glanced at the clock for the first time that afternoon. I had missed the flight by two hours.

The winds of fate were seemingly lifting us ever upwards and by the time the album had come out and we were making our first transatlantic forays 'Animal Nitrate' had become a proper top ten hit. My sly ambition of firing a poisonous missive into the heartland of the mainstream had happened as the song reached heavy saturation levels on Radio 1, the DJs seemingly strangely oblivious to the meaning of the words which were murky and twisted to say the least and to the obvious reference to narcotics in the title which perhaps was so blatant that it managed somehow to 'hide in plain sight'. It's amazing what you can get away with singing when you have a pop hook and so slowly it wormed its way into the public consciousness: parasitical, malign and very hummable. I'd once heard some probably apocryphal rumour that Kate Bush's 'The Man With The Child In His Eyes' was about masturbation, which seemed inherently artful given the lush sonic context and that idea had sparked a train of thought in me. For me though again the real treasure was on the B-side in the form of a song called 'The Big Time', my attempt at a dissection of the consequences of fame, a kind of sober tale of those left behind in its wake. I was beginning to see this happen in my life and writing it resonated strongly with how I saw things unfolding around me. Becoming vaguely successful myself didn't mean that I started making friends with other success-ful people. In a way the opposite happened as I buried myself in the comforting blanket of old, familiar faces like Alan and Tamzin Drew, feeling that they repre-sented something I could trust – something that wasn't capricious and unpredictable and always shifting. My close friends were on the dole or worked in chip shops or as menial office factotums so of course the whole change in dynamic occasionally began to create if not an uncomfortable differential then definitely an odd imbalance and it was this that I was exploring in the song and later in a way with 'High Rising'. 'The Big Time' was received by the press as our homage to Scott Walker but it's interesting that neither Bernard nor I had at that point any real knowledge of his work. J. G. Ballard references also kept cropping up as compar-isons to my lyrics when again at that point I have to ashamedly admit that I had never read him. Maybe these influences had bled through to us in other ways but maybe sometimes artists aren't always 'referencing' other art even though in the wilderness of mirrors that is our post-modern world it's probably more convenient to file it that way. There's a phenomenon in zoology called convergent evolution, a situation whereby two different species will evolve independently of each other into a very similar animal but by following different routes, and I think this can be paralleled in art.

In that time-honoured way the single had launched the album and the album had hastened to number one and sold rather well and all of those things that we had longed for had come true. I'll always remember the moment I told Simon the news. It was a Sunday afternoon and we were on tour in the UK staying at a hotel in Leeds or somewhere. I banged on his door to tell him we had a number one album to find him hunched over the little sink in his bathroom wringing out his smalls like Widow Twankey. It was a hilarious moment, an odd clash of glamour and drudgery, somehow bathetic and funny at the same time and strangely symbolic of an inherent contradiction at the heart of the band's character. We were soon to learn though that achieving your goals is never the end point that it might seem before you embark on the journey, and with an unslakeable thirst you begin to believe that there are always more units you can shift, more territories you can tame. With the hunger of an addict you find yourselves unwittingly set on a treadmill of repetitive behaviour, continuously chasing increasingly bigger fixes to satisfy the need for success, better chart positions, more effusive reviews. Our personal greed was always for that elusive next song, chasing them around the room like silvery, mercurial butterflies, but when not achieving what the industry expects somehow amounted to a sort of public shame we became forced to become complicit cogs in the huge tired machine. And the machine ground on. We were packed off on endless jaunts around the country which fed into European tours and then eventually American ones and that, as boringly predicted by many a self-satisfied observer, is where things began to unravel.

We only had a two-single deal with Nude and so we'd been to the States a few times as guests of record companies trying to sign us for an album deal and had spent hilarious stoned afternoons being rocked by pony-tailed man-baby record execs in hammocks in Malibu beach mansions or being picked up in ridiculous stretch limos in Manhattan, dazzled by promises and offered obscene amounts of money. In LA we were staying at the Mondrian Hotel on Sunset Boulevard when in the small hours we were awoken by an earthquake. For anyone who has never experienced anything like that it really is the oddest sensation which I can only describe as a kind of confusing terror. At a very primal level you know there's something you should be scared of but at first, before your brain has processed the feeling, you're simply not sure why. My abiding memory is of waking up to the room rattling and rushing down the emergency exit to the lobby in my T-shirt and pants to find Simon already there fully dressed and packed. Apparently Bernard had been so confused and panicked that he had called up our manager's room to tell him to 'make it stop'. During this period the chase for our signatures had become so frenzied that at one point an A&R man followed us to New York like a B-movie spy and checked himself into the same hotel in the hope of 'bumping into us' and bonding, eventually debasing himself by offering to sell T-shirts for us at one of our gigs as a desperate means to gain some sort of access. It all became a bit silly, a little like the Artie Fufkin scene in *Spinal Tap*, but we managed to preserve a healthy disrespect for it all despite the novelty, seeing the whole thing for what it really was – a frothy, ephemeral hysteria that was more to do with hard business than any flattering interpretation of our work. The only member of this increasingly bizarre cast with whom we felt any real kinship was a softly spoken intelligent New Yorker with a kind manner and enormous eyelashes called Kevin Patrick who at the time worked for Warner in the States, the sort of man who had a genuine wild-eyed passion for music but who would insist on finding stray cats to which he would feed the scraps of his lunch. Kevin has stayed a close friend of the band over the years and when we bump into him his is always still a trusted voice.

Lengthy tours are truly challenging experiences – they will stretch the limits of your patience and endurance and they will test the boundaries of the relationships between you and the rest of the band. It's a strange blend of insanity and routine, the releasing of bestial urges and the need to rigidly obey timetables. Partly because of its sheer scale, but mainly due to the cultural disparities, for a certain sort of band touring the States has always been seen historically as a particular ordeal. The Sex Pistols famously imploded in San Francisco in the seventies and I think many observers correctly drew parallels between us and them, wondering how the hysteria both bands were used to in the fiery crucible of the incestuous British music scene would translate to the larger, more disconnected ambivalence of the American one. To be honest though most of the shows we played there were wonderful, not just those on 'the coasts', which of course always have a special cachet, but also those further inland. There was a fervent throng of followers who would trail us from show to show and the whole procession took on a kind of carnival feel and, just to put the record straight despite the popular misconception, we always enjoyed playing America and the debut sold remarkably well there. However the more time we spent there the more Bernard especially seemed to become increasingly homesick and unhappy. Maybe somehow America distorted the reality of who we were to him and presented us as a cartoon of ourselves: greedy, fame-hungry and insensitive as we discarded the vestiges of sobriety and jumped through the industry hoops not particularly because that was who we were but because that's who we needed to pretend to be as a kind of means to survive the whole grinding, harrowing ride. As Samuel Johnson once said: 'he who makes a beast of himself gets rid of the pain of being a man'. Interestingly I don't think it was until we released the album and the band had the lyric sheet in their hands that they really knew the details of what I was sing-ing about and what kind of band they were actually in. Of course I was never evasive about disclosing the lyrics if they wanted to know but they rarely did and seemed to trust me and allow that side of the work to be exclusively my business. General themes must have bled though to them I'm sure and occasionally they might say, 'Oh, I like that bit' or Simon might jokingly paraphrase something but we weren't the sort of band who sat down together and talked about 'the meaning of our lyrics' in a self-conscious way – we just let things happen and didn't bother questioning them especially if everything seemed to be going well. As soon as the album was released however, as well as all the themes being revealed, a whole other layer of reinterpretation was presented to them via the response of the press and the fans. In a funny sort of way you yourselves are to a certain extent told what kind of band you are at this point in your career and occasionally it can be a bit of a surprise. I think Bernard was becoming particularly uncomfortable with some of the darker, less wholesome themes that were being exaggerated by the media's thirst for prurience. Added to this an increasingly 'foppish' – for want of a better word – element of our band and I suppose especially my character was being teased out and reflected back at us. It didn't help that I'd naively done a couple of ill-advised, light-hearted press pieces in which I'd stupidly played up to that: the dandy, the overtly English popinjay. Mistakes like this I deeply regret as these archetypes are so powerful that they can take on a life of their own and end up becoming overwhelming and extremely unwelcome strands of your image – inescapable, almost Jungian embodiments.

Perhaps now is the moment to talk about person versus persona.

PERSON VERSUS PERSONA

In pop music everyone becomes a cartoon: a fiction-alised version of themselves partly constructed from truth but partly something that complies with a simplistic archetype. This is a phenomenon that has fascinated me over the years, that chasm between the real you and the projections of others. I realise that like anyone in my kind of work over time I have had built up around me an image, a nebulous carapace made up from sub-editors' headlines and half-truths and rumours and so some might choose to see me as distant and aloof, arrogant and vain. I think that to be honest I have been partly complicit in its manufacture – 'the devil has the best tunes' they say – and so the furtive whiff of danger that it projects seems to blend with something inherently dark in the songs and I realise that of course in order for it to exist it must contain elements of truth. This simplification is part of the system that allows the public to file overwhelming amounts of information, to see things without the distracting shades of grey that reality requires. Sometimes though the persona develops a life beyond you and your control and like some sort of haunted ventriloquist's dummy in a bad horror film it will feel like the real you is being smothered and suppressed by the imposter. If this sounds melodramatic and whinging it's not supposed to – the contract that you sign when you first choose to wield a guitar or jump on to the stage is very clear and anyone who fails to read the small print waives the right to complain about it. I'm not going to bother pleading a case for myself as some sort of wholesome, square-jawed, misunderstood hero because that would be inherently reductive too but I do think it's important to note that real people are by definition more complex than their accompanying personas might lead you to believe. In literature I've always been drawn to those protagonists, like Stephen Wraysford in Sebastian Faulks' *Birdsong*, who sit somewhere within the myriad shades of grey, somewhere between the binary simplicity of cosy polar certainty. In pop music, however, it can be a difficult territory to occupy. The whole subject of the persona in pop is a compelling one. No one who steps foot on a stage or gives an interview or even sings a song is free from its manufacture on some level. It's a necessary device to allow the individual behind the mask to somehow be free to be more themselves than if they weren't wearing it, and in order to have the bravery to face the crowd. The artist Gillian Wearing did some interesting work on the subject whereby she encouraged strangers to confess their fears and terrors but from behind the protective anonymity of a costume mask. It allowed the participants to be free to express themselves without there being consequences for the 'real' person. There are parallels with what happens to the pop star: whether it's conscious or subconscious the persona is a way for the vulnerable human being that is always hiding behind the brittle shell to protect themselves from the storm of perversity and distortion of reality that they will inevitably encounter and again for the consequences of their frankness to not affect the 'real' person. People might condemn the whole process as 'fake' but it's as fake as the act of stepping on stage or singing a song which is of course both a kind of fiction and a kind of truth. In the same way that many bands who believe that they are consciously rejecting the notion of 'image' by not 'dressing up' are unwittingly therefore projecting an image of 'anti-image' so the manufacture of a persona is unfortunately inescapable and is something that the artist willingly embraces and accepts or will struggle with for the rest of their career.

I think in my case I was very much guilty of a naive complicity during that early period when my persona was still being lovingly woven and adjusted by the media. Of course it seems ill-judged now but if I'm honest I probably chose to view the whole process as titillating, secretly deeply flattered that people seemed to care about who I was or seemed to be, regardless of whether their vision was a misrepresentation or not. Years of poverty and struggle and failure had made me hungry for any scraps of success that were thrown my way and in my frenzy to feed I think I was often far too willing to indulge their silly fantasies and wear the costume that was being so carefully stitched for me despite the fact that it increasingly seemed ill-fitting. Unlike artists from the past – the Dylans, the Lydons, the Bowies – I don't think I was ever particularly in control of the manufacture of my persona. Unlike them I wasn't smart or aware enough at the time to be able to see what was happening and so it seemed to be something I was perpetually either embracing or distancing myself from, caught in a cycle of assent and rejection. I think that very few artists can be consciously in control of it without it coming across as unscrupulous and somehow fraudulent. One of the tenets of nineties alternative music was to portray yourself as 'authentic' so that bands within that genre were distanced from the gaudy, artificial sensibilities of the seventies and eighties. Whether this actually was the case or not was beside the point but like so much about pop music the issue is how things appear to be rather than actually how they are. I realise that discussing it now with this kind of clarity implies that personally I had some sort of manipulative ability but if I did it was deeply subconscious, the young man that I was blindly stumbling around just letting things passively happen to him. These strange forces that were exerting their pull on me and the almost violent sense of flux that I was experiencing were undoubtedly having an effect on my private life. Everything was far too unsettled and exciting for me to even think about stable relationships as I staggered between bizarre dalliances and sticky, gaudy dramas, my private life becoming increasingly odd and rootless. For a while it felt like I was trapped inside a Futurist painting, restless and kinetic as I ricocheted around locked within a strange new dissonant version of reality.

Once these early mistakes with the media had been made we learned the cast-iron rule of never having fun with the press; what seems like a laugh at the time will always come back to haunt you and be used against you – but by this point the damage had been done. Really we should have had the wisdom to realise that not all exposure is good exposure but we didn't and while we were still riding the crest of a wave it seemed somehow churlish to bother questioning it as it buoyed us along. To be fair all of us hated this severely mutated interpretation of who we were; it was probably responsible for a subsequent two decades of overly humourless press photos, but Bernard seemed most bothered and unable to deal with it, seeing it, I think, as a direct contradiction of who he was and of what he believed Suede to be. All of this was feeding into his sense of discontentment and when we started playing America and the rest of the band dived into the temporary bestial release that touring can offer, Bernard preferred to stay in his room on the phone to England, increasingly isolated and removed from us. It didn't help that my friend Alan flew out to California to join us on the West Coast leg and the natural hedonist in him exaggerated that in me creating an additional disparity and I suppose he occupied the vacancy of 'my best friend' on the tour leaving Bernard's and my relationship further neglected and in need of care.

Damaged and exhausted but still functioning we eventually flew back to England for a while, but the pressure to 'break' America is an overwhelming obsession in the music business and so we were soon blithely packed off on another transatlantic flight. This time tragedy struck. Bernard's father, who had been ill for some time, died on the eve of the tour. Ashen-faced, we all received the news while in a hotel in New York. For some insane reason instead of cancelling the tour and giving him the time to grieve and the space to try to recover we just truncated it. It was a terrible, terrible mistake as Bernard became understandably more and more withdrawn and distant as the days wore on and I, yet to develop the emotional maturity to be able to reach out and comfort him as a friend, began to cravenly hide within the excesses of life on the road. As we pulled in different directions our relationship began to splinter and we began to demonise each other creating a chain of events from which we would never ever recover.

PART TWO

THE POISON TREE

As the 747 touched down on the tarmac back at Heathrow the familiar sight of damp grey airport concrete greeted me through the tiny porthole window of the plane as little droplets of English summer rain beaded against the glass. There was a gnawing sensation in the pit of my stomach and as I finally approached the trickle of black cabs that beetled its way along the road outside the terminal I felt that quiet dread when you know something is terribly wrong, that sense of unfixable shift, that cold sink of animal fear. The American tour had spiralled into a fractious, unhinged display of passive aggression and latent hostility, separate travel and on-stage sulks. It was a masterclass in how relationships can descend into disorder, the bonds severed, the parties irreconcilable. This is the soap opera that the press and the public find so exciting: to know that there is genuine human emotion behind the artifice of what is essentially manufactured feeling, to know that the music has at its core real passions and real fears and real dramas, to know that it's not all just pretty words. By this point it was almost impossible to just pick up a phone and call Bernard. In my eyes he had mutated into a slightly terrifying figure – angry, irascible and unpredictable – and in that cowardly way that people with those options sometimes choose I communicated with him via the buffer of our manager Charlie whom we saw as a solid, reliable figure within the maelstrom of madness that had become our lives. Bernard himself of course was probably equally confused and intimidated by me as I hovered on the fringes of stardom, self-obsessed and greedy for success and increasingly insensitive to the nuances of anyone else's feelings. The distorting lens of the tour had painted us to each other as those garish cartoons of our real selves, polarising us as people, exaggerating our differences and turning them into almost unbroachable schisms. The only thing to do was to not do anything and so for a while we all slumped back into the familiar shape of our old everyday lives with that strange sensation that lengthy tours can create when eventually you return; a feeling of both comfort and displacement, an institutionalised state of not quite being able to fit back in but of not having the energy to do anything else.

Especially when they are young musicians often

speak to each other most fluently through music. It provides a conduit that allows them to express themselves in abstract ways, sometimes to vent and to rage but to do so within the safety of a set of codes. So eventually once the dust had settled we rebuilt those scorched bridges by getting back into the studio and working again, by gingerly stepping inside the same space and in a hesitant, circumspect way striving to do what we did best. The next project was planned to be an interim single. We'd written a song called 'Stay Together', an unambitious rock-by-numbers chug-through that for some reason seemed to excite us at the time. Looking back, the only thing that lifted it out of the ordinary was its sheer length and the bizarre mainly instrumental second half of the song which shifted through various moods and phases and contained snippets of a ranting spoken-word piece I had written that was loosely based on Patti Smith's 'Birdland'. This whole section was I think Bernard's Expressionist collage, his wild howl of fury and grief and pain and frustration, his violent catharsis, his primal scream, his hymn to alienation. It was an attempt at expressing himself in the medium in which he was most eloquent – sound – and as such I think it was brave and ambitious. But for me the song itself was very much below par for us and lyrically it was anodyne to the point of meaninglessness: a collection of tired Suede-by-numbers urban landscape clichés and second-hand emotional posturing. It's possible of course that subconsciously the title was a plea to Bernard, an appeal to my friend as I saw him becoming increasingly alienated and estranged from the rest of us. I don't remember being aware of that at the time but looking back it can't have been a coincidence and I know many people would wryly chuckle at the irony as events began to unfold. Perhaps if I had really confronted my own anxious feelings and been honest enough to allow myself to explore that theme more fully in the lyrics the narrative wouldn't have ended up being the unexceptional afterthought that it became.

Throughout this whole early phase of when we first became popular we were continually hounded by accusations of 'hype'. It was a predictable knee-jerk reaction by those who felt that our seemingly rapid ascent was undeserved. When 'Stay Together' smashed its way, unformatted, to number three in February of 1994 I'm afraid for the first time I was inclined to agree that the haters had a point. I remember thinking it sounded lumpen and inelegant and for me it has grown no less unsightly with age. Yet again the B-sides were where the real jewels were hidden: the delicate, understated melodic drama of 'The Living Dead' and the possibly even stronger 'My Dark Star', a deceptive and in many ways seemingly unremarkable, mid-paced piece which somehow on repeated listens manages to continually reveal deeper layers and has gone on to deservedly reap minor adoration. Lyrically the latter was a strange song, an attempt to stretch myself as a writer beyond the arena of personal emotional drama and to start to sketch on a broader, more political canvas. Trying to make sense of it will probably make it sound somewhat 'New Age' and unfocused and possibly a bit sixth form but it was a song about the power of the feminine – an odd vision in which a strong messianic female leader, who I based loosely around the artist Frida Kahlo, emerges from the shadows of the Third World to take over the reins and steer us all away from the brink of disaster. There was a vague thread running through my writing at the time that hinted at a naive suspicion of authority which you can hear in the lines about 'the lies of the government's singular history' and I suppose the references to India and Argentina were deliberate in that they pointed at countries that had at some time been crushed under the heel of Britain's imperial jackboot. Occasionally songs have a magic that is more than a sum of their parts. There's a popular perception amongst a certain sort of member of the public that pop and rock lyrics are 'childish' and 'immature' and 'vacuous' and they offer as proof the fact that when intoned just as words away from the context of the music they sound hollow: '*baby, baby, yeah, yeah, yeah* – what a load of rubbish' etc., etc. The whole point about rock and pop lyrics however is that, unlike poetry or prose, they are sung not spoken and as such their musical context is everything. I can't count the number of times when I've been sitting in the back of a cab over the years and been genuinely surprised and moved by a pop song as it has come on the radio, by some trite anodyne platitude that when delivered with feeling and melody assumes a state of genuinely Keatsian truth and beauty, transcending its ordinary components to reach beyond itself. Now, as the writer of 'My Dark Star', it's not my place to say whether the song achieves this or not, but my point is that isolating lyrics is not a fair way to judge the piece, merely a convenient one, because they seem to speak the same language as the medium which is describing them. Therein lies the whole 'writing about music is like dancing about architecture' paradox – the inability of one medium to in any way accurately express the other.

By this point Alan and I had left the flat in Moorhouse Road and were now residing on the ground floor of a large Victorian Gothic house on Shepherd's Hill in Highgate. It was a move that tied in with my growing fascination with the number sixteen as every flat and house I had lived in since relocating to Kensington had had that number and it was very much a desire to temporarily retreat from what I saw as the urban scurry of west London into a leafier, more secluded environ, a refuge from the shrill chatter and the cackle of rumour and the constant procession of hangers-on. From the street the house seemed dank and crepuscular with cantilevered bay windows and mock-medieval pillars, set back from the road and veiled by privet and plane trees: sober, solemn and imposing. But at the back of the house the double-height French windows in the living room opened on to a beautiful, long, south-east-facing garden that stretched away from the house and was dotted with apple trees and bordered by low yew hedges. It was owned by a Christian Anabaptist group called the Mennonites and the whole place was somehow imbued with a strange ecclesiastical ambience and thus wonderfully odd and completely removed from the commonplace bohemian bustle of Notting Hill. My and Alan's reckless lifestyle hadn't changed much though and we would often be slumped on the sofa in the debris of the night before, lost in the babbling labyrinths of excess when suddenly the strains of pious singing would bleed through the walls as the Mennonites went about their hymns or recited their prayers creating a bizarre clash of worlds: the dissolute and the devout meeting at last in a garden flat in N6. Previously the places where I had lived had very much informed the songs I had written but with the flat in Highgate it was more than that; I think it began to inform a new persona I was subconsciously drawing for myself. The 'cheeky Cockernee chappie' role that had at first been offered to me by the press, and that I had obviously rejected, was now being happily inhabited by groups of witless, opportunist Mockneys – middle-class 'media geezers' who had learned to drop their aitches and flatten their vowels – so I was keen to distance myself from what, in our wake, was now starting to become a movement. The interpretation of British life that we had initially sketched and that I saw as being more akin to a Mike Leigh film was now being twisted into a *Carry On* film, with all of the fragility, poetry and pain removed: an ugly vehicle for latent nationalism and sly misogyny, a cheap, beery, graceless cartoon bereft of passion or rage which cravenly hid feeling behind a brittle mask of irony. Despite having nearly destroyed us, our exhausting touring schedule had presented me with marvellous world experience and access to places that were way beyond the reach of most kids brought up in council houses in Haywards Heath and I was keen to embrace this rather than retreating back inside the cosy, parochial *Dad's Army* world that was becoming the central cultural reference point. I started to read about witchcraft and became obsessed with figures like Lewis Carroll and Kenneth Anger and Aldous Huxley and with classic Hollywood icons and their macabre, tragic lives. I began to gravitate towards a certain sort of creative mind – odd, idiosyncratic seers like William Blake and Aleister Crowley whose muse was harder to label and define – delving into their muttering, veiled world of symbolism and incantation. Lost to a vinous blend of chemical experimentation and lurid, ego-driven derangement I would pad around the flat dressed in nothing but a kind of long, black, gold-braided Moroccan robe, scribbling down phrases and gathering ideas, throwing things into the cauldron and watching them boil.

So this was who I was becoming – the person with whom Bernard and the rest of the band were now confronted – a damaged, paranoid figure, wired and isolated, edgy and obsessed and lost within a strange fantasy landscape, a simulacrum of life. When I look back at press photos from those days I can't help but feel the palpable sense of enmity between us all, the current of discord, the feeling that something had permanently snapped. Something unfixable. It's most apparent in our body language in the inner gatefold 'Stay Together' single-sleeve photo of us all in the car, the shoot for which I remember being a particularly tetchy affair: fraught and prickly and unpleasant. Bernard and I never really recovered any sense of unity and despite a perfunctory muddling through of promotional duties it was performed through gritted teeth, the unspoken bitterness always on the point of resurfacing. I have a strong memory of feeling like I had to tip-toe around him very carefully, fearful of reawakening a simmering, bilious persona and plunging us all back into a strange, dark theatre of tension. Had I possessed the maturity and clarity to just sit down with him and clear the air 'man to man' things might have been very different but it had moved beyond that point and

I stupidly didn't because I simply wasn't able to and so the wound festered and spoiled and grew. It's possible that I was projecting my childhood experience of those anxious years spent dealing with my father's brooding moods on to this situation, that the increasingly charged, irascible atmosphere between Bernard and myself was echoing those uncomfortable moments I had spent as a young man walking on egg-shells around my dad and that consequently I was starting to view Bernard in a similar light – as someone for whom I cared a great deal but with whom I shared a complex often contradictory relationship that at any minute had the capacity to flare up. To promote the 'Stay Together' single we had organised a small string of dates which culminated in Edinburgh's Queen's Hall. Although we didn't know it at the time it was to be Bernard's final concert with Suede; fittingly a fractious, bad-humoured affair which was peppered with silences and uncomfortable pauses as tempers frayed and cables malfunctioned. By this point it was quite clear to me that Bernard's time in the band was effectively drawing to a close and that, sadly, it was just a matter of when not if.

THE ONLY THING THAT'S SPECIAL ABOUT US IS WHAT WE LEAVE BEHIND

Young men plunged into the crucible of success are by their very nature immature and instinctive and impetuous. These are the fiery ingredients that also spark drama and creativity and the thrilling imbalance and sense of potential disaster that make the spectacle so exciting to witness. Without this essential 'flaw' in their characters the whole thing would be far less interesting but of course it's a precarious house of cards, always teetering on the point of collapse. Sellotaping over the cracks and disregarding the damage we spluttered on regardless. Blithely I lost myself in the comfort of writing, secretly praying that somehow, magically, given space the wounds would heal on their own. Looking back this seems more than a little hopeful but I lacked the life experience to understand that a passive approach like this was unlikely to do any good and I was finding it increasingly hard to accept the wise counsel of anyone around me who had my ear. I think I had personally arrived at a unique point in my life that in many ways mirrored the position in which we found ourselves as a band. The enormous success of the debut album had exaggerated my sense of self-confidence, distorting it into a kind of brittle hubris, making me at times unapproachable and seemingly self-contained but often actually vulnerable and confused. The appearance of confidence was of course just a mask I wore, another element of the persona that was being constructed around me, partly by myself and partly by others. It's an essential tool that any and every performer needs but sometimes it can interfere with things, distorting your perception, forcing you to make bad judgement calls, making you think you are above and beyond advice. Again it's all part of the myth of the artist in which people need to believe. The role of the assured, confident seer 'leading his children, Moses-like, to the promised land' was a trope that flushed with the arrogance of youth I naively felt I needed to emulate. Indeed when it eventually came to deciding upon the first single for the new album I vividly remember the head of Sony, our international record company at the time, almost begging us to let them release 'New Generation', seeing it as the 'radio-friendly unit-shifter' of legend. The poor man wheedled and reasoned and pleaded while I just sat there in the boardroom with a face like a clenched fist and told him that the single was going to be 'We Are The Pigs', an uncompromising, jarring epic that was completely out of step with the shifting zeitgeist and which was eventually welcomed by the media like a letter from the taxman.

Between dates and during sound checks we had been slowly chipping away at new songs; Bernard's wonderful, restless drive being, as ever, the motor that drove us on, stretching us ever beyond the limits of what we thought we could do and on to new roads, always reaching up, always finding another gear. The broken relationship was too delicate to risk a face-to-face encounter, the powder keg too close to the sparks that might fly, so we began the slightly strange, dislocated process of writing by post. Every week or so a yellow Jiffy bag containing a cassette tape would be pushed through my letterbox and flop on to the doormat, laconically biroed with a series of working titles like 'Trashy' or 'A Man's Song ' or 'EAG' or 'Ken', and I would pick it up and wander over to the small writing room which I'd made on the north side of the house and slot it into my blue Tascam portastudio and sit there, my SM58 poised, to listen and ponder and sing. There's occasionally something wonderfully meditative about writing; the sense of being confronted with yourself and your own thresholds can be in many ways enlightening – that thrilling chase, that breathless pursuit, the feeling that the solution to the puzzle is almost, almost within your grasp. I suppose writing songs was the way that Bernard and I had always communicated; spurring, goading, inspiring, challenging and when all the other channels had shut down there was an odd feeling that despite the unconventional way in which we were doing it there was something pure and unfettered in the simplicity of having stripped our relationship back to its central purpose. Within the beautiful, fraught music he was sending me I was sensing pain and sadness and frustration and drama and I knew it was my job to match and mirror those feelings, to reflect the kaleidoscope of his emotions but to do it within the context of its own narrative. Both of us knew the next record had to be very special – it felt like the success of the first demanded it – and so we steeled ourselves to push beyond the outskirts of our ability, to take all of the rage and paranoia and fear and love and pour it into the songs, to make the highs giddy and vertiginous and the lows desperate and chilling. If this was to be a swan-song then what a way it would be to end it all.

The first track that we had written was one that had been knocking around for a while, since at least the tail-end of when we were writing the debut but we simply couldn't fit it into the rock format of the band, choosing instead to perform it on a couple of occasions on TV and at Glastonbury as a simple acoustic vocal and guitar piece. The definitive arrangement still eluded us but we knew the song was strong enough and that if we could get it right it would be a powerful closing piece. It was called 'Still Life' and it was the second chapter in my 'housewives saga', the first being 'Sleeping Pills' on the debut. It was a tale in which the abandoned, yearning protagonist waits at the window for their errant lover, lost in pools of melancholy reflection, partly inspired by my mishandling of my split with Justine but also of course conceived as an attempt to inhabit the mind of my mother during my childhood: isolated, trapped and desperate. Those sentiments of dislocation and alienation became one of the main themes on the album and were to bleed poisonously into many of the songs including notably the other big, blousy ballad 'The 2 Of Us'. One of my most vivid memories of Bernard as a musician was watching him play the stirring, plaintive piano part through the control-room glass at Master Rock Studios. As I sat there spellbound while he poured his pain into the keys I felt one of those rare, searingly beautiful, life-marking moments, something that I will never forget: a strange humbling blend of pride for our work together and of sadness for what might all be soon to end. The track became another anthem to alienation – the story of two people in the world of high finance joined together but unable to connect, their empty, loveless lives ironically spotlit against the steel and glass back-drop of their apparent success: 'alone but not lonely, alone but loaded'. The parallel with my and Bernard's position, even though not at the time consciously intended, has over the years revealed itself to me as possibly its true meaning, but like I have said before, songs will often slowly and mysteriously uncover themselves, even sometimes to the writers.

Another of the early tracks that we had been road-testing on the 'Stay Together' mini-tour was 'Heroine'. As soon as Bernard sent me the pounding, pushing arpeggio piece it stirred me enough to want to write something straightaway. I loved the dark, winding minor chords and the almost Gothic motifs that inter-twined and swirled and surged. Sitting working on it in the house in Shepherd's Hill one winter day while the rain washed in waves against the window pane I remember a strange sensation of its dank, serpentine phrases reflecting the very nature of the place, the masonry and the cement somehow coiling within the fabric of the music, sinuous and malevolent. The obvi-ously homophonic lyric was one of which I am most proud and which for me has resonated quite neatly as we move further into the virtual landscapes of this century. It is a vignette of a porn-addicted adolescent lost within the lurid pages of his magazines, unable to reach out into the real world, shamed and impotent and isolated – a state with which most young men, if they are honest, are somewhat familiar, the lewd promise of feminine flesh tormenting them from within the processed colour pages of *Penthouse* or *Mayfair*, or these days from within the soft luminescence of their laptop screen. This idea initiated an extension of the alienation theme: real people bonding to fictional characters and fantasy figures. I saw it happening in my life and in the world around me where friends were being replaced by characters in soap operas, lovers with pornographic models and patriarchal role models with film stars. It wasn't a particularly new phenomenon – young men had been borrowing the body language of matinee idols for decades – but as the twentieth century heralded the coming of the twenty-first it seemed to be increasingly relevant and thus insinuated itself to a greater or lesser degree into many of the other songs. The opening line of 'Heroine', which I borrowed from Lord Byron, was one of those kinds of 'cut and paste' moments where I would sometimes throw random ideas plundered from the pages of my notebooks at a song to see whether they scanned. The resulting jarring mix between the ancient and the modern worked for me, somehow suggesting a sense of continuum, an intimation of the timelessness of the challenges that we all face.

During endless drifting afternoons in the house I sat for many hours reading about Brando and Dean and Monroe, and staring at those beautiful, old, silver-gelatin fifties Hollywood prints I found myself lost so deeply in their superficial sheen that it became almost impossible to really see them just as it's hard to be in any way objective about such iconic images, their familiarity somehow overwhelming and blinding. It struck me that, clichéd and overused and over-familiar though they were, they had become almost a synecdoche that represented society's obsession with stardom, and so referencing this whole Hollywood machine and the stars that it creates seemed a further extension of my central thrust of alienation through idolatry. The song that delved most specifically into this was something Bernard and I came up with towards the end of the writing period called 'Daddy's Speeding', an odd, creepy little piece, part song, part sound collage that detailed a dream I had had about James Dean and which touched on themes of tragedy and immortality. Another track we had also been road-testing was initially called 'Trashy'. A thrilling, pulsing, riff-based beast in 6/8 time it was brilliant to play live: visceral and urgent, brimming with a gnarly, powerful violence. Although the working title was strangely apposite I renamed it 'This Hollywood Life' and into it wove a story set in the tawdry world of the casting couch, a garish tale of ambition and sexual exploitation that I suppose mirrored what I had glimpsed happening in some of the murkier corners of the music industry. For me though the song that sat like a jewel in amongst the others was something that began life with the prosaic title of 'Ken', jokingly so named by Bernard after the only other person who had answered the *NME* advert through which we had met him. Working titles became a light-hearted dialogue between us sometimes and he would deliberately give things names like 'Unusual Sex' just so we could have silly conversations like 'I really like "Unusual Sex".' 'Yes, so do I.' etc. etc. 'Ken' was a rootsy, mid-paced, initially quite conventional-sounding track with an easy, fluid, almost Gene Clark or Jimmy Webb sort of feel, which I first remember Bernard playing in a sound check in Phoenix or somewhere on one of the early American tours. Its unpretentious, stirring power seemed to be something I should go with and not try to subvert so I wrote a part very much inspired by Jaques Brel's 'Ne Me Quitte Pas' and of course more specifically Scott Walker's English translation which I was learning to love. Throughout this whole period I was starting to listen to the 'big' singers from the past like Sinatra and Brel and Piaf – performers who could transform a song into a drama – and I tried to take something from them and stretch myself as a musician. I was keen to evolve beyond the scraping, nasal drawl that had covered most of the debut and find a differ-ent voice, still my own of course but one which would resonate better with broader, less parochial themes. It was this new approach that I brought to what (obviously referencing Marlon Brando) I had called 'The Wild Ones', the song that I would still choose if I was forced to nominate just one single moment in my entire career as a writer that says: 'This is what I have done with my life.' I have a vivid recollection of writing my parts to it and realising that something very special had happened and then stumbling out on to the wintry rain-lashed streets of Highgate and striding around coatless in a kind of deranged, euphoric daze, oblivious to the weather, lost in a delicious solipsism and probably risking pleurisy. The sad thing is that the great songs are rarely the successful ones, certainly at least in the narrow band of experience that has defined my career. It was to become a bitter illustration of the meaninglessness of chart 'success' given that the vacuous Suede-by-numbers chug-through 'Stay Together' had reached number three on a wave of hype while 'The Wild Ones' limped in and out, barely scraping the top twenty and coinciding unfortunately with the moment when our star began to wane.

As well as widescreen ballads we were still writing wiry pop, the best of which was probably what became known as 'New Generation'. It had been another track that had been working well live for obvious reasons; its driving, almost motoric groove and two-part soaring chorus giving it a classic pop/rock feel in the same sonic world as someone like The Pretenders or the rockier bits of Blondie. As is often the way with good pop songs the lyrics were a little throwaway to be honest. I recall that it was vaguely inspired by my watching from the sidelines what was happening to Justine and her new band Elastica, seeing them begin to break through with their brilliant, spiky, off-kilter art pop. It was meant as a song of love and encouragement for her, the bitterness forgotten, the scar tissue healed. During a sulky, bad-tempered few days of pre-production at a tatty rehearsal room in Dollis Hill we had also been chipping away at a track that had a kind of straight rock feel akin to something like Neil Young's 'Ohio'. It was called '10 Minutes', a working title which referred to its length. Back in Highgate I had written some lyrics and melody to Bernard's primitive demo but as yet the song hadn't come alive for me. Somehow a little clunky and ordinary, it felt good but not yet great, and Bernard's insistence that it be a long and meandering piece that shifted through different tonal gears seemed incommensurate with its seemingly underwhelming character. How wrong I was. The lyric I wrote has become one of which I am most proud – a tale of three-way sexual jealousy inspired by my relationship with the previously mentioned artist who during the fractured chaos of our loosely tethered time together had begun an affair with another woman. The song was a meandering journey that followed her, stalker-like along the leaf-scattered pavements and through the overcast day, prying into the complexities of her life

113

and her loves, myself cast more as an observer than a player in the drama. I love the way the meaning holds back and takes its time, eventually revealing itself with the lines 'she's got a friend, they share mascara I pretend' and suddenly the story is upon you. I called it 'The Asphalt World' and it was to become one of the most loved songs in the Suede canon, but before it became the track that people hear today it underwent huge shifts and within the band turned into a controversial touchstone that seemed to somehow embody the growing schism between Bernard and the rest of us. Now there is some difference of opinion about the specifics here and I'm trying to remember the truth rather than what has assumed the shape of the truth in my head, but I do remember bad-natured tussles in the studio about the song's length where Bernard insisted it be deliberately overlong and the rest of us baulked, worrying that it would come across as grandiose pretension. Looking back, he quite rightly knew that the drama would only be unlocked by a bold, almost reckless musical gesture and had complex plans to fill the spaces with intricate guitar parts and stormy, dramatic mood shifts. He was totally justified in pursuing his vision of course but as always the problems lay in the delivery and interpretation, in my reaction and in his counter-reaction, a consequence of the erosion of trust and respect between us. We pushed and pulled and the song nearly broke us but eventually we had something we could all work with – a brooding, simmering leviathan, a dark hymn to suspicion and sexual jealousy.

This artist also featured heavily in the track 'Black Or Blue' that was to precede 'The Asphalt World' on the album. She was a colourful character to say the least, fitful and wild and unpredictable, her turbulent moods inevitably hiding a sensitivity at her core. Sometimes she would come to my house and just sit around quietly drawing on her sketch pad while on other occasions she would do deranged things like put bricks through my window to wake me up. One summer evening she came to the house in Shepherd's Hill in an unhinged state and ran on to the south-facing lawn and proceeded to roll around on the grass screaming. A neighbour must have called 999 because suddenly uniformed police were at the door obviously concerned that she was being attacked. Once they had begun their questioning however she decided to shift the focus of her rage on to them and it was all I could do to try to calm her down so she didn't end up spending the night in the cells. I didn't have the maturity at the time to do anything more than dismiss her behaviour as perverse but looking back there may have been some troubling forces at work. The relationship was highly unconventional; fraught and sometimes passionate and fragmented by my increasingly skewed lifestyle. Certainly in no way was I a candidate for standard boyfriend material, my kinetic, shifting world far too unsettled for the relationship to become anything other than transitory. Somehow though the inherent dissonance at the heart of it formed a strange kind of bond between us, both of us covertly accepting the perversity as part of the deal, and there must have been something between us to have yielded songs with the quality of 'So Young' and 'The Asphalt World' and 'The Wild Ones'. I remember feeling at the time that my relationship with her was beginning to echo both that with Bernard and that with my father in so far as all of them had become in some way highly confrontational. It's probably true that this was just as much a reflection on the prickly, unpredictable person I was becoming as I ricocheted around the fringes of stardom, pinballing between the 'real' me and the strange, fragile persona I was beginning to inhabit. Oddly for me 'Black Or Blue' is a vaguely underwhelming piece that seemed to step over into the unwelcome fringes of pretension. It was intended as a kind of *Romeo and Juliet*-style vignette set in a modern context of racial intolerance; the lovers melodramatically torn asunder by the narrow minds of those around them etc. etc. The artist's family were from an island in the Indian Ocean and ambling around the streets of Gypsy Hill together we would occasionally encounter witless racists directing moronic comments at her and at us but rather than letting them eat into me I allowed the poisonous asides to grow into tendrils that inspired the lyric to the song. Despite coming from an interesting place I don't think the sentiment really rescued the track as it struggled to come across as anything more than an amuse-bouche before the main course of 'The Asphalt World' and would have rendered the album much stronger had it done the decent thing and stood aside for the brutish thug anthem that was 'Killing Of A Flashboy', another in a long line of rather decent squandered B-sides.

Inspired by things like 'The Hounds Of Love' and 'Closer' and 'The Spirit Of Eden' we had always intended the album to be an ambitious sonic journey for which of course we needed a starting point. Bernard had written this odd, mechanical runt of a piece which he called 'Squidgy Bun'. At first its crushing, metallic drone seemed incongruous to our song-based style but as I sat there at my portastudio and allowed its churning, pulsing waves to wash over me I began to understand its potential role in the record. Instead of being a song in its own right it began to reveal itself as a kind of prelude and I went about writing a simple, layered almost monotonous mantra rather than a conventional piece. It was very much inspired by a visit I had made to a Buddhist temple in Kyoto during a Japanese tour when I had become lost in one of the monks' cyclical, hypnotic pieces and I saw the potential for it to mirror something like that. Inspired, I went about writing a kind of relentless

Orwellian chant that sketched the journey of an imaginary band, a restless marching machine that trampled over continents in its pursuit of power. In the same way that Sergeant Pepper's fantasy band is a role played by The Beatles so this song contained elements of how I perceived Suede's journey but hugely exaggerated; extended and distorted out of proportion and made into an almost nightmarish cartoon. When I think about this track I'm always put in mind of O'Brien's comment to Winston Smith telling him to imagine the future as 'a boot stamping on a human face – for ever' as it has something of that relentless, inhuman brutality. I called it 'Introducing The Band' and it was to end up being the opening piece on what will always be for some people, admittedly frustratingly, the band's high-water mark: *Dog Man Star*.

WE LOVE, WE TIRE,
WE MOVE ON

As the dirty grey canal water lapped gently against the sides of the Feng Shang Princess floating Chinese restaurant the four of us gathered on the tow-path of the Regent's Canal, murmured a few words of recognition and shuffled into the garishly themed interior to take our places for a drab photo shoot. Inside a few small groups of lunchtime diners were already huddled around their dim sum and large orange oriental lanterns lit up the corners of the room with their lambent glow, illuminating the little warrior figurines and dragon motifs which decorated the space. Although we didn't know it at the time, this odd gaudy stage would turn out to be the back-drop for our final scene: the last time we were ever all in the same room together. Across London towards the scruffy end of Kilburn High Road between the Chicken Cottages and the shops advertising 'Cheap International Phone Calls', and nestled behind the black wheelie bins and the car parks lay Master Rock Studios, the charged arena of tension and invention hosting the fraught, sometimes inspired sessions for *Dog Man Star*, this line-up's final album together. The days and nights had taken on a kind of iambic pulse of their own, a natural rhythm whereby like passing trains Bernard and I would occupy slots at different ends of the day, him choosing to work away on the complex maze of guitar overdubs during the mornings and afternoons leaving me to waft in vampirically under the cover of darkness and begin the night shift. Ed was of course thrust into the middle of our fractured dynamic, forced to mediate and absorb the obvious disquiet, charged with the thankless task of attempting to somehow glue the broken pieces back together, or at least to not make things worse.

Diplomatically of course Ed would always soften the blow when relaying anything back but the picture that was bleeding through to me was of Bernard feeling trapped and claustrophobic and extremely unhappy within his role. It was very apparent that he no longer seemed to particularly like the band that he was in. My response was I suppose a mixture of anxiety about what was to come and waves of frustration and sadness and gnawing feelings of betrayal, my emotions oscillating and my moods mutable, but these feelings were sometimes tempered with an odd hubristic charge, a strange sense of welcoming the welling sweep of change that seemed now so inevitable. I suppose it was with this fatalistic veneer that I presented myself to the rest of the band and the management and the record company at the time – an illusion of insouciance and control – but privately I was devastated and scared and without the maturity to be able to admit to that. It's hard not to let the soap opera of my and Bernard's splintering relationship overwhelm the story of the album as it seems so consuming, a huge smothering, unignorable element in its genesis. Such dramas frame the work which they generate within a tangible human context, lending the essentially abstract art form of music a more concrete element. They give it a back story, a lens through which people can view and inter- pret the songs. However looking beyond the ubiquity of the affair there was also quiet, sober work to be done and despite the stormy relations we had a record to make. By this point Ed had I think very much learned to trust us as artists and had reached a more hands-off approach when it came to our songwriting, allowing the quality of the work to steer the record. I suppose this was partly because despite the personal drama we were as writers enjoying what Neil Tennant once called the 'imperial phase' – that magical period when a band has mastered itself and can seemingly do no wrong, before it feels the need to question and reinvent, when the work is instinctive and its momentum unstoppable. This was at the core of my frustration: what should have been energy we were expending on creating and improving and growing was wasted on what seemed sometimes like petty, unnecessary infighting and I couldn't help but feel a kind of churlishness about the fact that having worked so hard to get to this point we seemed to be on the brink of blithely casting it away. There were moments of seeming cohesion of course – Bernard's bravura piano performance on 'The 2 Of Us' and his eternally inspiring musicianship and restless quest for perfection – but it all seemed to be covered in a thin layer of prickliness, a miasma of anxiety, a heightened awareness of shortened fuses and a sinking, sour inevitability.

I'm finding this chapter particularly hard to write. It isn't pleasant raking over this episode so hopefully you'll forgive me if I stray towards any mawkish hand-wringing but it's so important for me to understand what went wrong and facing it head-on with as much honesty and clarity as I can muster is the only way I can do that. I am often tormented by moments of reflection in which I plot an alternate version of history where I have the bravery and presence of mind to confront the problems rather than hiding under the brittle shell of my persona and the shifting gossamer layers of mercurial success, but unfortunately I didn't and untended the wounds continued to fester. One day on my way to

Master Rock to put down the vocal for 'The Asphalt World' I picked up a copy of the now defunct *Vox* magazine in which Bernard had been interviewed. I know very well how publications can take words out of context and suggest certain meanings by what they decide to highlight but even seeing through the mechanics of media distortion the piece did come across as the ravings of an especially unhappy man who had chosen me in particular as a target. It was an unpleasant diatribe in which I was cast as unmusical and slow, a slightly inept, shallow inversion of the purity and brilliance of Bernard's musicianship. To be fair he did personally apologise to me a few days later in a forced, mumbled encounter orchestrated by Charlie but by that point it felt like the damage had been done. He had been naive to allow this very public criticism to be teased out of him and seized on trophy-like by the press and it did feel cruel and shaming. I understood of course that it was a raw, brutally frank expression of frustration but somehow it seemed to step over the boundaries of what should be kept private which deepened the unavoidable sense of betrayal and inevitably acted as a spark that lit the tinder-box. This might come across as ironic given that I am myself so publicly laying bare the private intricacies of the episode here but this is *my* way of expressing and assimilating some of the hurt and confusion that I still feel from this whole chapter. Having just read the *Vox* article I delivered my vocal to 'The Asphalt World' with the pain still stinging, the bitterness and the rancour swirling around as I sang my troubled tale of jealousy and suspicion. Hopefully I was able to channel that into the song, and I like to think you can hear it in the iciness and the drama, a sour embodiment of the maxim 'pain is temporary but art is for ever'.

As well as directing criticism at me Bernard was becoming increasingly vociferous about what he perceived to be Ed's shortcomings. At this juncture I should point out that it seemed very much that Bernard was increasingly isolating himself and rather than the fissures being just between him and me, the camp seemed to split into two distinct groups: Bernard on one side and everyone else on the other. I think that whenever people can be bothered to look back at this episode it can often conveniently be seen as a simplistic clash between him and me; the tragic, romantic narrative of the two warring writers being sometimes too seductive to resist – a neat embodiment of how they sometimes choose to interpret the polarity of creativity and its inherent contradictions. The truth however is that as time wore on it felt that in his frustration he was picking fights with everyone, kicking against the entirety of the band itself, but that as its leader I was somehow representative of its 'evils' and so bore the brunt of his disquiet. To be honest I'm finding it hard to remember the sequence of events, and I might be wrong, but it seems unlikely given the fracturing of our relationship that Bernard and I sat down and sensibly discussed his production issues. Instead his discontentment bled through to me via a series of barbed asides until it reached a crisis point where in an acceleration of events he delivered an ultimatum forcing us to choose between firing Ed and losing him. In the dying afternoon light of a bleak north London day Mat, Simon, Ed, Saul, Charlie and I gathered sombrely in a flat in Belsize Park to try to make some sense of this vertiginous turn of events and after a solemn few hours of discussion the phone was passed to me and down a crackly line I told Bernard that our decision was to keep Ed. It wasn't that when I made that fateful choice that I was actually choosing Ed over Bernard, merely that I was refusing to be bullied in what came across to me as a childish power struggle, a way for Bernard to wrestle back some influence as he drifted further away from the band. I don't know what he thought my response would be but it has struck me that it was possibly his subconscious way of allowing himself to exit or at the very least his way of forcing me to make that choice for him. By this point I honestly don't think there was anything anyone could have done to convince him to stay long-term – giving in to his demands would have merely been delaying the inevitable as he was obviously extremely unhappy and deep down I think he just wanted out. This struck me as the only real option: a damage limitation exercise that might at least allow us to complete the album rather than the violent, destructive collision that it felt like we were plummeting towards. It seemed that responding to his ultimatum was in a way like responding to an act of terrorism in that if you cave in to it you create a precedent that will lead to a complete relinquishment of control. Could Ed's technical handing of the album have been better? Probably, yes, and I think he would be the first to admit that but surely it was something that didn't require such a confrontational, binary approach. The decision that I took that day in calling Bernard's bluff was, for better or for worse, a truly life-changing moment and one that will continue to haunt me for the rest of my days.

ANYTHING CAN HAPPEN IN
LIFE, ESPECIALLY NOTHING

The live room of studio one in Master Rock was bathed
in the shadowy glow of dull red forty-watt bulbs and
as the drifting coils of incense smoke snaked through
the air we three remaining members of Suede sat at
our instruments and began to play. I fumbled inexpertly around the first few jazzy piano chords and
Simon skipped along breezily on his kit while Mat's
playful bass part held down the bottom end. After
the end of the instrumental verse I began to sing, my
reedy unamplified voice lost in the cavernous room,
thin against the thump of the instruments: 'Tall and
tanned and young and lovely.' We were playing 'The
Girl From Ipanema'.

During the first few days following Bernard's departure we were all quite honestly filled with a strange

sense of elation, a feeling that a crushing, smothering weight had been lifted from us. The fractious conflicts of the preceding six months or so had been a truly horrible experience – enervating, draining and more than a little unpleasant – and so the visceral surge of relief following the lifting of this weight was in a way intoxicating. Of course, like a cheap high, the sensation was short-lived and essentially artificial, and lurking behind the brittle relief there lay uncertainty and doubt. I suppose I hid my feelings of betrayal and confusion beneath a thin mask of professionalism believing that the only way I could negotiate this daunting hurdle was to be seen to be approaching it as just a minor hiccup but what choice did I have? Bernard clearly was very unhappy and no amount of leaden self-reflection was going to bring him back to the fold and so I ignored my inner dialogue and continued in the only way that I knew how, by throwing myself headlong into my work. Sadly by this point our former friendship was in such tatters as to just be a memory but still within me there lurked a shadow of grief for the loss of someone with whom I had shared so much and with whom I was once so inseparable. I often reflect on the circumstances that led Bernard and me to this point of estrangement especially when we had always been in our own unique sort of way quite close. It's tempting to see conflict between oneself and someone else as being the 'fault' of the other person but hopefully with a quarter of a century's distance from the event we have both moved beyond that simplistic impulse and can look at the circumstances that directed us both there. It's more than possible that fame and success and money distorted the natural differences in our personalities. Although it's a character trait of which I'm not particularly proud it's certainly true that during those early days especially I was often ruthlessly ambitious. The lean, gruelling years of struggle clambering up the bottom rungs of the ladder had given me a steely kind of resolve and so when we did eventually start turning heads I think I grasped any success that came our way firmly with both hands, anxious that the indifference that had met our career up until that point would resurface; the abject fear of poverty that my penurious childhood had instilled in me making me desperate never to return to that state again. Bernard on the other hand had different concerns and was I think always much more suspicious of the pitfalls and traps that lay in wait, in many ways secretly fearful of becoming too successful, rightly seeing it as a path littered with casualties and peppered with disillusion and bitterness. As time drew on I developed a singer's propensity for craving the spotlight whereas continuing good fortune seemed to stimulate the opposite response in Bernard who I believe saw us becoming something that he wasn't comfortable with – a band that was reaching too far into the mainstream and betraying its alternative roots. Looking back there was a lot to admire about his perspective but unfortunately as young men we weren't really able to rationalise and explain how we felt about these things and so the schisms grew and the misunderstandings simmered and the differences widened. To be fair we were possibly all on some level damaged by the distortion of truth that we were being subjected to but I think that Bernard especially found it harder than the rest of us to let the whole thing wash over him, choosing to view it as pernicious. Unable to resist kicking against it, I suppose on some level he felt a bit isolated when the other members of his band didn't seem to see it the same way. I think he always had a much more puritanical approach than the rest of us. Whereas we were all willing to let the fickle tide of fame and fate drag us along he was always more circumspect and often mistrustful of those who worked with us. His cautiousness was in hindsight commendable in many ways and emotionally very astute for someone in his position but for Mat and Simon and me the whole procession of madness was perhaps something we just felt we had to dive into almost with a suspension of disbelief, knowing that of course no one emerges unscathed and that the journey will only take you somewhere if you allow it all to engulf you and surrender to its dizzying pace.

Once Bernard was set adrift from the band our relationship would deteriorate even further as we sniped at each other through the safe haven of the press. Of course we were still too naive to realise that journalists would be hoping for exactly this and would of course be artfully teasing out and exaggerating the acrimonious drama during interviews, turning the sad truth of our estrangement into a cheap, gaudy soap opera knowing that it made great copy. I regret not having had the grace and restraint during this period to have just maintained a dignified silence as it meant that inevitably we became further embittered about each other and that what was once a friendship that had such a noble purpose and that had created so much beauty had descended into a spiteful, petty, public squabble. It would take almost a decade for us to finally be able to approach each other again with any vestige of civility, the legacy of that long feud compounded by the ugly machinery of media distortion.

The odd sense of initial release merged into an in-between transitory sort of time when Ed and I were confronted with the task of finishing the record but without one of its chief architects. Apart from issues over the length of 'The Asphalt World' which was easily solved with a tape edit (in those days manually performed with a Stanley knife, a chinagraph pencil and some adhesive tape) there were other musical differences that now we were free to address. Bernard had wanted 'The Wild Ones' to have a long coda part – a completely new section that appeared unannounced

at the end of the song like a kind of *deus ex machina* –
but both Ed and I felt it contradicted the pop heart
of the track, dragging it into a more avant-garde territory where it just didn't feel comfortable. Making
the stark executive decision we removed that section
and replaced it with a looping, fading reprise which
although definitely less challenging seemed to chime
with the easy beauty of the song. We added some
sound effects to strengthen the sense of journey in the
record: a twisted, distorting saxophone part fading
into the guitar intro of 'This Hollywood Life' and a
sinister *Lord of the Flies*-style chanting children's choir
at the end of 'We Are The Pigs'. There were some
ideas that didn't work. Ed had this strange obsession
about recording a tap-dancer to build up a rhythm
track for 'The 2 Of Us' and even went to the lengths of
hiring someone to perform the part, providing a surreal moment for me as I watched through the control
room glass as the poor man desperately, and ultimately
fruitlessly, chased Ed's bizarre vision. It summed up his
off-kilter, often eccentric approach to making records,
something that was both lovable and infuriating and
which provided the ammunition for many years of
good-natured leg-pulling.

The only song that we had written but not recorded
was something called 'Banana Youth', a big, billowing,
rolling, mid-tempo ballad. When asked to pick out
the themes of the album in the predictable interview

questions that followed its release my stock answer became: 'It's an album about ambition and aspiration'. This massively inaccurate slice of personal PR bullshit was a shame as it failed to highlight the truer, darker themes of disintegration, alienation and dislocation in an attempt to put on a brave face and confront the obvious career uncertainties with a brittle, smiling mask of optimism. It was probably only really this track, which I called 'The Power', that actually fitted that remit. As is often the case with new songs the recording of 'The Power' was carried along on a wave of buoyant enthusiasm, and in an act of trying to embrace a new sense of unity we recorded the drums, bass and acoustic guitar as a three-piece live in the studio and then later hired a session player to mimic Bernard's electric guitar parts from the demo. Looking back I think the inclusion of this track was a mistake – it contained none of Bernard's gnarl and grit and always just seems lightweight and incongruous next to the rest of the album, like a child in a restaurant who has accidentally joined the wrong family's table.

In an attempt to solve one of the trickiest of the album's conundrums, that of the arrangement of 'Still Life', we took what at the time seemed like a radical decision and decided to orchestrate it, hiring someone who had worked on a couple of Scott Walker records to write a score. I think the basic idea was right but the execution was hugely overblown and in our naivety we managed to lend the song an unwelcome air of neo-classical pomposity when a more understated arrangement would have let the internal drama of the song breathe more. It's so easy to become seduced by the sheen of professionalism that a large string section can lend a track – somehow you can see it as a kind of validation of your work that lulls you into believing that you're enhancing it when in fact you're often doing the opposite. By the time we had got to CTS studios in Watford to hear the forty-piece orchestra play along to our little song though it was all too late and had cost too much money and it seemed kind of churlish to point out what was niggling me then and has grown more apparent ever since. Unfortunately I feel the overpowering orchestration effectively ruined what is such a moving song, and it's something that I refer to, in a cautionary way, to this day when negotiating similar situations. I wish we had had the bravery to take a simpler, more 'honest' approach but we were young and ambitious and maybe these are the kind of mistakes that you just have to learn from. While all this was happening Bernard himself was in a studio in a different part of London quietly laying down some guitar and keyboard overdubs to 'Black or Blue' as a fulfillment of his contractual obligations, allowing him at last his longed-for freedom from the band.

Completing the album gave us something tangible to grasp hold of but still the strange, dark summer of uncertainty lurched on and the novelty of the situation began to slowly mutate into a kind of quiet panic as we were forced to plot our next move. There's always been something quite bloody-minded about the Suede ethos: if people expect us to do one thing then we will do the opposite and there's a willingness to reject and confound, a mischievous refusal to comply. So when the world and his wife were telling us that we were finished our reaction was to decide to carry on. The problem was that we had never been one of those bands who really hang out with other bands. The London music scene had very quickly become unin-teresting to me after a brief initial dalliance and my mild social anxiety had developed into a fully formed neurosis now that minor fame and major narcotics had wormed their noxious, invidious way into my life and massively distorted my ability to judge the reaction of those around me. I think I possibly possess that classic personality trait where people mistake the distance and removal that I orchestrate through a natural shyness as a haughty arrogance. It was this lack of connection to any network of fellow musicians that made it harder for us to look for a new guitarist as the simple fact was that we didn't know any. We have never been 'musician's musicians', I think we are possibly too arch and seemingly too ambitious and aloof to be so. It's an aspect of our group persona which has in a way paralleled my feelings of 'not belonging' socially as a child in that I have never felt much sense of kinship with other bands. I also think that there was a desire to do things in an unconventional manner, to eschew the channels through which these processes usually operate, so instead of calling up Gary Moore or holding big, revealing public auditions we ended up asking a completely unknown teenager to be our guitarist.

One day while chatting with Charlie over some milky tea in his offices in Provost Street I was rifling through some post and I came across a yellow Jiffy bag containing a cassette tape and a short letter. It was from a young man called Richard Oakes who was randomly offering his services as Bernard's replacement. Admiring his chutzpah I slotted the tape into the stereo expecting to be confronted with a quiet display of underwhelming amateurism. What I heard however as he ran through a version of 'My Insatiable One' was a stirring and eloquent performance, lilting and nuanced and obviously technically extremely proficient. Equally excited, Charlie called the number in the letter which turned out to be that of Richard's family home in Poole. After a lengthy conversation with his mother it transpired that Richard was just seventeen and still at sixth form. Initially this fact worried me, and looking back it was a little rash not to be more worried but the more I thought about it, the more the perversity appealed and trusting my instincts we arranged for him to travel to London for an audition. As he trudged into the rehearsal room in Southwark, despite his fresh-faced youthfulness and the strange disparity of the situation, Richard seemed confident and friendly but refreshingly unassuming. He was a smallish kid with long, dark straight hair which gathered into a widow's peak and a handsome, hawkish bone structure that has always reminded me a little of a young Dave Gilmour. We drank tea and exchanged pleasantries but once he'd taken off his coat and plugged in his guitar his obvious talent seemed to transform him, strangely inverting the power differential and making him seem like the master and us the novices.

Richard is the most naturally gifted musician I have ever worked with. He has an eerie ability to hear things and pick things out in music of which I'm simply not aware, let alone able to play. Over the years his uncanny ability has often made me ponder Schopenhauer's famous maxim 'talent hits the target that no one else can hit, genius hits the target that no one else can see' as his understanding of music has always been bordering on the abnormal, so different from the stumbling, haltered journey that I had to personally undertake. In many ways I think he was possibly too technically proficient, the fluidity of his playing coming too easily to him and denying him the struggle and the lessons therein that most of us have to wade through. Music for me is a very instinctive thing – I try to let my ears do the work and let my brain sit back and rest – so hearing

Richard playing with us that first time I knew that we had found the right person. Of course we knew we would be faced with years of meticulous work during his assimilation as we tried to bridge the gaps presented by the age difference alone and all of the myriad complications that it might throw up, but in Richard I saw a raw talent, a seed that given the right conditions could grow and eventually bloom and flourish so we decided to take a gamble. It's possible that by appointing Richard I was unwittingly orchestrating a power play of my own: wresting further influence over the band by replacing a dissenting, challenging voice with one that I saw as being acquiescent and compliant and easy to mould into a convenient shape. I'm sure it probably came across like that to some people. Honestly I have no recollection of that being a conscious train of thought but the machinations of one's own mind can be veiled even, and sometimes especially, to oneself. The seemingly untold months of unbearable friction with Bernard had definitely snapped something in me and so a desire, conscious or otherwise, to steer things differently was certainly lurking.

Having no real choice but to shove Richard roughly and heedlessly into the deep end we organised a couple of shows. The first of these was at a grubby little club in Paris and then another at The YMCA just off Tottenham Court Road. Both were desperately riotous affairs, sweaty and deafening with the throbbing energy of a band emerging at last from stasis and self-doubt. In my excitement I probably over-compensated for his inexperience but he accounted for himself well, carrying himself with an assurance that has been his hallmark ever since, seemingly oblivious to the pressure that everyone else thinks he should be feeling. When I asked him about this he told me that it was just that he had such poor eyesight that he couldn't even see the front row, let alone what was going on beyond that, so the whole visual experience for him just passed by as a strange, unintimidating abstract blur. Years later when he eventually bothered getting himself contact lenses he told us that the first gig he played wearing them was truly terrifying, confronted at last by the sea of animated faces to which for years he'd been oblivious. We moved him to London into a shared house with amongst others our good friend Mike Christie. We'd met Mike when he was working with Derek Jarman after we had approached him to direct a promo video for 'So Young' back in the spring of 1993. Tragically by then Derek was dying of AIDS and had moved into the latter stages of that awful, fatal illness so simply couldn't commit but Mike had steered us towards working with two of Derek's students, David Lewis and Andy Crabb, who had also ended up directing a series of films we had commissioned for the *Dog Man Star* tour to be projected behind us as back-drops and which Mike had produced. Over the years Mike has become a dear and trusted friend – loyal, perceptive and often unnervingly intelligent and always great fun to be with – and he has worked with us and become part of our family, following our vicissitudes and living them alongside us. He promoted the fiery, charged show at Blackpool Tower Ballroom just before Bernard left and would end up wasting much of his young life making incredibly strong coffee and listening to us moaning on tour as well as of course going on to direct 2018's *The Insatiable Ones* documentary. Richard then callow, inexperienced and provincial was plucked from the cosy safety of his family and thrust into the bubbling metropolitan cauldron not only of the capital's rock demi-monde but also of the gregarious London gay community, almost like Pip in some updated, highly modernised version of *Great Expectations*. Again his quiet calm, his refusal to be seen as being bothered, steered him through as we accelerated him unnaturally and possibly slightly recklessly through the gears of life.

As part of Richard's continuing baptism of fire we embarked on an endless, gruelling programme of touring, our limits narrowing to the relentlessly rain-washed windows of the tour bus and to the strange daily rhythms of catharsis and clock-work order, release and routine. On his first visit to Tokyo he was confronted at the hotel by a throng of obsessive fans and a brace of tiny, very chaste-looking Japanese girls holding an enormous banner hilariously emblazoned with the words *FUCK US RICHARD*, possibly the result of a translation miscommunication. In Hamburg while the rest of us cavorted drunkenly and embarrassingly around the flesh-pots of the Reeperbahn we locked him in his hotel room with an acoustic guitar and jokingly told him that he wasn't allowed out 'until he had written a hit'. Amazingly, instead of just telling us to fuck off he responded with the music that was later to become the song 'Together', the first sign that there might be a creative life beyond Bernard. As the tour rumbled along the motorways of Europe we were forced into the intimacy of each other's lives and became close-knit and mutually purposeful, smoking together, listening together, laughing together, planning together: a tight little team made tighter by an ever-growing siege mentality. We were very much aware of a louring storm that was gathering, a building rumble of discontentment in the press which, given other options, was choosing to see us as increasingly irrelevant: a 'dead band walking', a group who couldn't possibly survive in any meaningful way after Bernard's departure. This was made all the more frustrating for us due to our inability to respond, trapped as we were within our mundane promotional duties, forced to tour an album that seemed no longer relevant to us and desperate to redefine ourselves as a creative force. Like any trial it was onerous and at times unpleasant but ultimately necessary. Richard wasn't yet ready to speak as a writer and his time marinading in our influence was an essential ingredient in what would become the next album. When I think about the demands that were made on him at such a young age it seems extraordinary to me that he didn't buckle and collapse. Apart from the technical feat of playing Bernard's parts he had to suffer the indignity of always being in his shadow, of always being compared and often not favourably. This was partly of course a natural consequence of his new role in the band but I think as well it had very much to do with his reserved nature: always understated, never showy, keen to reject the florid rock clichés that the press so secretly love. I think he realised very early on that there would be no point in competing with Bernard's enormous persona and so instead chose to quietly go about his job, something that he is still doing today. I think over the years that there have been consequences from the initial disparity in our relationship. It was always going to be an extremely tricky balancing act finding the right levels of encouragement needed to bring him up to speed when he was so much younger than us. His extraordinary technical ability went some way to bridging the gap but I worry that sometimes over the years I may have allowed my frustrations with peripheral matters to boil over and bleed into the dynamic of our relationship and I'm sure at times he may have started to see me as a kind of authoritarian 'teacher' figure rather than the friend and bandmate that I always wanted to be. I ponder a lot the question of whether I have allowed him the space to grow out of the shadow of Bernard and become an artist in his own right while at the same time being doomed to subtly try to guide him and shape him into someone who has some of Bernard's undeniably fine qualities. Richard once brilliantly described joining Suede as 'the best thing that ever happened to me – and the worst'. The wry aphorism perfectly sums up the conundrum of his predicament: it was a role that he could never refuse but simultaneously one in which it would be almost, almost impossible to succeed.

When *Dog Man Star* was released it was to rapturous acclaim, the press recognising in it the work of a band that had dared to leap beyond its limits and stretch into new, unknown places, but everywhere there was a niggling undertone, a querulous subtext which of course wondered how we could continue when what was seen as our creative force had been wrenched away so savagely. The mutterings of disquiet continued and the public confidence in Suede began to wane, coinciding not coincidentally with the new wave of bands who waved flags and dropped their aitches and painted a social tourist's cartoon of British life: patronising, jingoistic and crass. The press's heads were turned and they followed like a child chasing a ball into the road.

PART THREE

EVERYONE WHO HAS EVER LOVED ME HAS BEEN AT SOME TIME DISAPPOINTED

The walls of the tiny box room were littered with Blu-Tack and random pin-pricked images of sixties pop stars and pages roughly ripped from magazines. On the white wooden painted frames that separated the orange-fabric sound insulation, sheets of lined A4 paper crammed with forests of manually typed words billowed gently in the artificial breeze from the electric fan. Outside it was a sultry summer day and inside the cramped, insulated, hermetically sealed writing room that I had had built in my new flat the air was unbearably close and oppressive. My shoes squeaked against the rubber floor and the sweat beaded on my forehead as I slotted a cassette tape into my portastudio and leaned into my SM58 to continue the seemingly Sisyphean task that is writing an album. Alan and I had moved into a bright top-floor maisonette in Chesterton Road, a scruffy, dog shit-littered street in North Kensington where rows of peeling, lower-middle-class Victorian houses had been badly hacked into flat conversions. It was just a few streets away from where I had first met Bernard on that fateful October evening in the late eighties and the flat was everything Shepherd's Hill wasn't: light, urban and charged with a breezy, bustling energy. It was a two-storey maisonette, so after struggling up the communal stairs you would first be greeted with the darkened, cramped floor that housed the bedrooms and the small studio. A further climb would reveal a large space dominated by a big, black L-shaped sofa which opened out on to a small, cheaply tiled concrete balcony facing westwards towards Shepherd's Bush and the Heathrow flight path. It was a lighter, more modern-looking apartment than the Highgate one which I always thought had the vague feeling of one of Hockney's deliberately unfussy seventies LA spaces, but still everywhere there were ash-trays laden with butts and Murano glass lighters and *objets* loosely arranged on the simple steel and glass coffee table around which we would gather and wile away our youth.

Most afternoons I would mutter and shout into my microphone and hammer away in a clammy, clattering frenzy on my typewriter interrupted only by the occasional member of Alan's burgeoning harem who confused and hungover and clutching their clothes would burst into the wrong room on their way to work while Alan lay comatose, still dead to the world, sleeping off the previous night's regular vinous cocktail of alcohol, narcotics and downers. The dank, labyrinthine opulence of *Dog Man Star* had been embodied by the house in Highgate and I had begun to strongly associate its looming Gothic arches and gloomy calm with the fraught dramas of my and Bernard's last few months working together so it had felt like it was time to escape its oppressive presence and scurry back to the cheery embrace of west London. Alan and I had picked up the same sort of dissolute rhythm we had developed in Moorhouse Road and the same sort of odd menagerie of drifters and dealers and misfits and girlfriends and the nights would often melt into mornings and the mornings into days and the days back into nights again while oblivious to the temporal shifts we would babble and smoke and chatter and shriek, the CDs and records scattering like a strange, shifting carpet across the sea-grass matting and then when everyone else had finally had enough and staggered back home, Alan and I would start all over again. Even though it might sound decadent and debauched it was all conducted fairly respectfully, still within a spirit of light, sociable hedonism, Alan's rakish charm firmly intact and always ensuring that the festivities never assumed a darker edge. In many ways Alan was the real 'rock star' in that house. He had the charisma and the looks and the leather trousers whereas I just sat sweating in my studio in my faded needlecords trying to write songs. The problem was he just happened to work in a chip-shop. I always used to feel sorry for his procession of lovers many of whom I would have to entertain while he was emerging from the depths of his hangover. Often they would bustle excitedly into the flat telling me about how they and Alan had plans to 'take a picnic to Kew Gardens' or 'go for a walk on Hampstead Heath', their pretty faces flushed with a brittle kind of gaiety that I knew would soon be shattered. These I used to call Alan's 'coke promises' as they were rarely, if ever, honoured and were one of the things that used to make me think that there weren't many situations worse than being reincarnated as one of his unfortunate girlfriends. Somehow though his lovable picaresque roguery always saw him through. Cat-like he continually managed to land on his feet, his transgressions forgiven as endearing peccadilloes, the disappointment forgotten as soon as the smile spread across his crumpled, handsome face.

At some point while shuffling around under the plane trees I'd met a girl called Sam Cunningham. She lived in a Victorian flat conversion on Lancaster Road just up from the library in a book-crammed room with a large south-facing bay window that looked out on to the street and a bizarrely outsize-panelled bedroom door that stretched almost all the way up to the double-height ceiling. She disguised her sensitive interior with a bright and funny manner and seemed somehow to be part of the very fabric of that part of London – the sort of warm, wonderful person who could and would chat to anyone and everyone in her perfect cut-glass English accent, smiling with her pale blue eyes, familiar and loved by the vast spectrum of people that, before the hedge-funders moved in, used to jostle and weave around the littered streets of Notting Hill. I would gaze on fascinated as chameleon-like she would give both market traders and minor aristocracy exactly the same levels of charm and energy, and of course why wouldn't she, but her deceptively easy mien came across as wonderfully unjudgemental and classless. I suppose on some level I saw in her an antidote to the intense, angst-ridden theatre that had seemed to characterise all of my relationships of late. We stumbled around the cracked concrete pavements of Ladbroke Grove together, dipping in and out of the pubs and the bedsits, her unpretentious ways bleeding into me and helping me shrug off the icy shroud of my Highgate persona. I wrote 'Sam' about her of course, a deliberately understated, very unSuede-like piece that tried to capture some of the eponymous subject's winsome charm with a similar one of its own. The little details about Lancaster Road and the library and the café where she would sip her tea were all real fragments of our world at the time, part of my attempt to develop, as Ian McEwan once so perfectly put it, a 'pointillist approach to verisimilitude', dusting the canvas of the song with little specks of truth. I remember coming up in the bedroom at Chesterton Road one hazy blur of an evening around the time when we first met while clutching a guitar, and the words and the chords and the melody just came pouring out of me in one of those uncanny and frankly untypical moments of songwriting serendipity. Even though in my mind it's strangely adrift from the Suede canon, too personal and sweet and lacking in drama to compete with the dark theatre of our accepted body of work, the song still speaks to me. It's probably purely a sentimental reflex but even today when I cycle past the library on the corner of Ladbroke Grove the little couplets of the verses still rattle through my head and I'm taken back to those precious, scruffy, beery days when we first met. 'Together' is another track that contains a lot of her presence. It was one of the first things that I wrote with Richard and as such it was an incredibly important tentative step on the path towards a new creative partnership. The song itself is a little snap-shot of the time when I first met Sam, playfully sketching the autumn day I bumped into her bouncing along Lancaster Road in a strange checked lumber-jack-style bomber jacket, her unwashed blue-black hair combed back and an impish smile flickering around her pretty face. In many ways Sam was unwittingly a huge influence on the vision for the new batch of songs that I was developing, revealing to me a warmer, sunnier world, less fraught but still charged with its own sort of thrill and romance.

By the summer of 1995 Suede was beginning to be seen as a spent force, at best an anachronistic punch-line or a cautionary tale and at worst an irrelevance. Somewhere, probably in the offices of *Loaded* or in a conference room in Millbank Tower, a party was going on and we were definitely not invited. As fashions marched forever onwards the taste-makers and the movers and the shakers had wandered away from us, interpreting our wounds as fatal and casting a bleak, cold shadow over our future. It was a hard time for me and it felt that the beginnings of a personal descent were somehow mirroring my band's as despite my attempt at the opposite I became prickly and irascible at the version of myself that was being projected by the press: that of a bitter, increasingly marginal figure who was never able to forgive the zeitgeist for drifting away from him. I was developing the classic trait that many people who have experienced a taste of fame exhibit: a childish secret desire to be noticed mixed with an instinct to hide away – a strange uncomfortable paradox born from the inherent insecurities that many who strive towards the public eye struggle with. It makes for an unpleasant sort of person: status-obsessed, vainglorious and brittle, always seeking validation for their own self-worth via how they think others perceive them. I tried to resist this suffocating, unlovable spectre but I would often find myself caught up within its noxious clutches unable to judge myself evenly and again oscillating between morbid self-reflection and unattractive narcissism. The only escape from this complex wilderness of self-doubt seemed to be writing songs; the one constant thread in my unsettled life and the only thing in which I have always been able to find sanctuary.

For a while Richard and I had been evolving a working dialogue – we had written a couple of things together which had turned out well and been good enough to use as B-sides but now we had found ourselves faced with the Herculean task of writing an album that would be the follow-up to *Dog Man Star*. The only way to confront the scale of the challenge was to ignore it and go in the opposite direction. It was vital to me, given that Suede was effectively now a new band, that we harnessed something of that vitality and irreverent freshness, that the new record took on the feeling almost of another debut because in a sense it would be exactly that. I realised it would be utterly futile trying to make *Dog Man Star 2*; that the white-hot chemistry which had created that album was born of a unique clash of forces, the shimmering apex reached through circumstances and experiences beyond the ordinary that could never be copied and that to try to do so would come across as utterly ridiculous and parodic and bound to be a bitter, inevitable failure. What I tried to tease out of Richard was a different treasure, something that I saw glittering within him: a simpler, less stuffy version of Suede, still both joyous and pained but rich with melody and instinctive, raw and jagged. Richard's musical loves were very different from Bernard's. He was a huge fan of the off-kilter, post-punk art rock of people like Keith Levene and John McGeoch and loved the wiry surrealism of the Fall but was still well versed in the classic sixties rock canon. I remember feeling absolutely certain that the record should have the crackle of energy that can only be made by a band playing together – that simple alchemy that four people with some bits of wood and some wires can create – the sort of thing that you might have heard before a million times but which always sounds fresh. The spectral, atomised way in which we had made *Dog Man Star* created something extraordinary, the broken shards and the splinters combining magically, but with this album I wanted it to sound like a band who enjoyed playing together, not the product of dislocation and estrangement. Writing with Richard was always going to be different from writing with Bernard. Obviously he was far less experienced and so I was very aware of my role as both mentor and co-writer, conscious of a disparity in experience but determined not to let that become something that inhibited him. Also I was keen to make him part of my little world, to usher him in and make him feel connected, aware that despite his self-contained manner he was still a young man who had been uprooted from the familiarity of his life and thrust into a strange new one. Alan and I used to often invite him over to the flat just to hang out and play the guitar and listen to music. When I mention it now Richard often reminds me that as an afterthought I'd often tack on a small shopping list of things for him to pick up on the way (usually cigarettes, cat litter and chewing gum) but the intention was always decent. I think he probably viewed us and our unusual life on the thresholds of propriety as secretly amusing but in his naturally unfazed way would come over and just kind of slot in around the chaos and the cigarette ash and the half-empty bottles, thrilling us with his guitar playing and doing hilarious impressions as he has an uncanny ability for mimicking people. He will sit back and observe you and tease out a tiny detail of your bearing or a verbal tic that you were unaware of and then project it back to you with a hilarious dead-pan delivery. Even those people who seem somehow characterless aren't immune. I often think that what was music's gain was comedy's loss.

One morning I was lying in my room drifting between sleep and consciousness when a simple, childish melody began to rattle around in my head, almost like a playground chant, circling and looping, niggling and insistent: 'Filmstar, propping up the bar, driving in a car it looks so easy'. I picked up my Dictaphone from the side of my bed where it usually lived and muttered the idea into it but it kept gnawing away at me and wouldn't let me get back to sleep. The only option was to see it through so I called Richard and hurried over to his basement flat in Kensington Garden Square just off the wrong end of Westbourne Grove. The morning had taken on an urgency so dispensing with tea and pleasantries I sat on his borrowed landlord's sofa and sang him my part slapping my palms against my knees to suggest the simple tribal rhythm I was hearing as an accompaniment. It was one of those rare, fluid moments in songwriting when everything seemed to fall into place easily, with an odd sense that the song almost already existed and it was our job just to capture it, like a photographer chasing the perfect image. Richard got it straightaway and began working on a gnarly, wiry, descending guitar piece that lent the whole thing a depth and complexity that previously hadn't been there. We needed a B-part, something that lifted the song away from its inherent chugging repetition so I started singing, 'What to believe in, it's impossible to say,' and Richard fitted some deceptively simple but effective chords around it and suddenly we had written 'Filmstar'. I liked the face-value, unveiled nature of the lyric: devoid of shades of meaning, simple and direct and forthright, somehow resonating with the superficiality of the subject matter. Later I wove in a little detail that suggested that the protagonist was more likely to be Alan Bates than Tom Cruise but the song remained essentially the same as the one we wrote together that day in Richard's basement flat as west London scurried and squeaked outside. It felt like this was a real watershed: suddenly I could see that there was a path ahead into the next record and that this song was leading the way. When we eventually recorded it I remember Boy George being in the studio next door and us press-ganging him and his band into participating in our 'handclap party', an event that Ed would often orchestrate to accompany the outros of many songs from that period. Without wishing to turn this book into a predictable avalanche of dropped names I've always liked George. He was sweet and generous to us when we skittishly and nervously pranced around on our first ever *Top of the Pops* in 1992 and you always remember little kindnesses like that. Bristling with a nascent confidence Richard and I tried the same approach as we had with 'Filmstar' with another half-idea that I had muttered into my Dictaphone one day. It was a sort of brutal, tribal chant based around the only drum beat I can play – a kind of simplistic Glitter Band beat/double beat thing. Again the idea only had one looping part when I leant on Richard's doorbell one grimy, sunless afternoon but lyrically it was slightly more developed. Even though she was unnamed in the song it featured another of my fictional characters, an extrapolation of the Terry idea from the early days. This character was called Sadie and she featured in a few of the songs from around this period but 'She' is easily the best. In this track I trailed her around the shitty backstreets of London as she made her way from bed to bed: predatory, heedless and beautiful as the night. I suppose it was another romanticised portrait of feminine power in the same sort of vein as 'My Dark Star' but with a grittier, jagged, cynical edge describing a high-heeled, highly stylised flaneuse, strange and 'terrible as the dawn'. In a repetition of our writing of 'Filmstar' I tapped out the childish beat on my knees and sang the words and Richard started threading a similarly knotty guitar line around the melody but this one for me was in a different league: a churning, plummeting motif with an almost Egyptian feel, not that I particularly know what Egyptian music sounds like to be honest but the part had an unusual exotic harmonic that somehow sat beautifully against the portrait I was sketching of disaffection and mutinous sexuality. Again it felt that, instead of a proper chorus, we just needed a simple B-part that shifted into a new gear so Richard suggested some chords which led to the 'nowhere places' section which then looped back round again unfussily to the verse. I finished it off by adding a falsetto *whoo-hoo* hook, an idea that was inspired by Howlin' Wolf's classic 'Smokestack Lightning' which I think may have been rattling around my head as it was being used in an advert at the time. Sometimes when these moments happen you are tricked into thinking that it will always be so but for better or for worse our writing has never been as carefree and simple again as during those leaden, grey afternoons in 1995 when we wrote 'Filmstar' and 'She'.

Every evening around this time tended to descend into a blizzard of narcotics and boozing, the flat a shifting stage through which a procession of misfits would wander. One such night a friend of mine Gary France and I had managed to get ourselves into a particularly ragged state and as the dawn broke over west London I grabbed a guitar and we sat looking out towards Shepherd's Bush drunkenly lurching into some tuneless singing. By the time the sun had come up we had written a batch of suitably comical songs with titles like 'Kisses For My Missus' and 'Santa Ain't A Wanker', but more than that a whole persona for the band that would perform them and even its name – Bruiser: an overtly laddish, almost Hogarthian caricature of a 'blokes' band, full of beery football chants and barely concealed misogyny. Although at the time it seemed hilarious it now of course just comes across like a silly drunken moment. The only reason it might be worthy of any mention is because I suppose it was my private way of ridiculing the scene that was becoming known as Britpop, a movement which we had propagated but with which we always had a very uncomfortable relationship ever since *Select* magazine had superimposed a Union Jack behind my image for a cover piece back in early 1993. While Richard and I were writing songs for the successor to *Dog Man Star* the scene was reaching ugly new heights of ubiquity and jingoism and cultural parody which I began to privately despise and possibly secretly feel responsible for and I suppose Bruiser, ridiculous though it was, was my way of venting and not allowing any of that bile to spill out and infect my work, ring-fencing the anger as the scene grew into the misshapen creature that we all remember.

Back in the real world Richard would busy himself writing ideas that were his own inception. One of the early ones he prosaically called 'Ballad Idea'. It was a beautiful, wandering, slow-burning piece, highly melodic and evocative and stirring but the chorus seemed to be too wilfully obscure. The rich, complex detail of music is something that I have always had to rely on others to provide but I'm quite good with the simple hook so I took his idea and replaced his meandering chorus with a basic D/E/A/F sharp minor chord sequence. It unlocked the song for me and suggested the tale of an everyday office girl looking forward to the weekend when her boyfriend would take her out.

I called it 'Saturday Night'. I suppose it was very much inspired by those wonderful, alcoholic winter London evenings that I had spent with Sam nursing pints in pubs and standing in foyers of cinemas and the tone was intended to be warm and embracing: a celebration of the simple pleasures of life. A couple of ideas of mine were solo pieces I had written way back in 1993 almost as a security against the seemingly not unlikely event of Bernard leaving the band. I had bought myself an old Stanton and Sons upright pre-war piano and somehow hauled it up the stairs to the flat in Moorhouse Road where I had tinkered and meddled, playing around learning chord shapes and melodic parts to things like 'Wuthering Heights' and 'Lady Stardust' as the cat slept curled up on the top and candle wax dripped over the keys. Not having the ability to go much further beyond them I tended to stick to simple, childish progressions one of which was the 'Puff The Magic Dragon' A/C sharp minor/D/E pattern. When I've written something I'm pleased with I'll often use it as a starting point for a new song and sometimes those starting points stick. It was around the time I was recording 'So Young' and the garbled intro shriek of that bled into the first line of the one I was writing at the piano: 'She can walk out anytime, anytime she wants to walk out that's fine'. I called it 'By The Sea' and it was conceived as a tender, wistful love song, a soft, yearning anthem detailing escape from the city to some fictionalised coastal idyll. If I'm honest I was thinking a bit about Justine when I wrote this and a similar little escape fantasy that we would occasionally allow to spool within our ragged, murmured late-night conversations but I was also very aware that the opening of the second line could have been interpreted as a reference to Bernard's departure. However, as I have said before, trying to pin absolute meanings to songs is in my mind futile – they breathe and live through different shades of shifting interpretations. Another childish ditty that I had written years ago back in the Moorhouse Road days was called 'Lazy'. It was a song about Alan and me and it painted a familiar picture of us flopped within the chaos of the night before, two perfectly happily isolated people bonded by their refusal to join the real world, watching in a furtive, circumspect way from behind the blinds as life jostled and scurried on the streets below. It certainly has a callow charm but it's hardly one of our best, rescued only by the brilliant melodic guitar part that Richard threaded through it, chiming and cascading like the line that Roger McGuinn never wrote.

CROUCHENDERS

The huge vaulted ceilings of The Church Studios in Crouch End echoed with the crack of Simon's snare drum as the guitar part to 'She' rattled around the room and the bass throbbed and droned. Endless, neglected cups of tea had cooled on the amps and sat there like sad little wallflowers, the stewed, cold liquid within them rippling as the room vibrated and shivered. The four of us were running through the track having been offered free time by Dave Stewart who owned the place back then and who must have taken a shine to us and been feeling philanthropic. We took a break and shuffled back into the control room grabbing our cigarettes and slumping heavily into the black leather studio sofas to listen to what we had recorded. Simon had brought a suit in with him on a hanger and had hung it on a coat hook on the door, vaguely muttering something about his cousin coming over to pick it up as he was borrowing it for an interview. As the menacing, grinding rhythms lurched through the NS-10s the door opened and a slight, winsome young man wandered in smiling a communal greeting above the din. His name was Neil Codling, the cousin who needed the suit, and the job he was to end up getting would be a very different one. Once the music had stopped and we started chatting it was clear that beyond the handsome face and the coltish fold of limbs there lurked a sensitive boy, inquisitive and well-read and possessing an easy kind of charm. Simon had neglected to mention that he was also a fine musician, an especially adept pianist, so as one of the songs we were working on at the time was 'By The Sea' I suggested casually that he jam along with us freeing Richard up to try out some guitar ideas. It was the first time that Suede had ever played like this as a five piece and the shift in dynamic from a quartet to a quintet felt wonderfully fresh and exciting and somehow in keeping with my desire for us to feel more like a new band that happened to share a name than just the same one with a line-up change. I don't really remember the point at which Neil actually joined the band – he just sort of hung around and became part of us. It was a wonderfully natural, almost serendipitous thing, unplanned and unpredicted and utterly right. As you climb your way up into the business end of the music industry your life takes on a repetitive, quotidian sort of feel, your days filled with events and rehearsals and appearances and shows, imprisoned within the narrow, biroed pages of your manager's diary. The chance occurrence of meeting Neil felt wonderfully free from that suffocating rigidity, like it was somehow preordained; an inevitable page in the script of our lives. And so we carried on with what felt right. Mat would pick us up in his tatty old bronze seventies Merc and we would putter up through Maida Vale and St John's Wood and Camden, chattering and smoking endless packs of Benson and Hedges, carelessly dropping ash over Mat's faded leather interior as *Never Mind the Bollocks* or *Revolver* or *Tanx* played on the cassette deck and north-west London disappeared behind us in the rear-view mirror until eventually we would arrive in Crouch End and begin work again.

One day Mat was tinkering around on the piano with a sweet minor-key chord sequence. There's something knowingly mechanical about the way he plays the keyboards, probably born from simple lack of practice but it's like he refuses to entertain the idea of being florid or overexpressive so his parts often have a kind of comically robotic, almost Florian Schneider-like charm. In his unassuming manner he was just playing in a quiet, almost meditative way to himself but I could hear something in the icy grandeur of the chords, something that suggested a sultry Berlin-period ballad so we played along and worked the song into a demo and jokingly called it 'Sombre Bongos'. I took it home and wrote a piece called 'Europe Is Our Playground', a simple love song that used the metaphor of travel to parallel the phases of feeling in a relationship, its flux and its change. It was loosely based around a trip that Sam and I had taken to Barcelona around that time, a wonderful few days prancing around the sun-kissed esplanades and piazzas, dipping in and out of the shaded side streets eating gazpacho and drinking cold beer together. When asked about the song I have often jokingly said that I intended it as an advert for Interrailing but my flippancy belies the fact that it's incredibly dear to me and I feel it grows in stature with each passing year, another in a long list of criminally underrated tracks that were consigned to the no man's land of the B-side. I distinctly remember a phone discussion with Saul about whether it should go on the album and for some reason at the time we both thought its surging, wintry elegance didn't fit with the fizzy upbeat nature of the record, something of a shame for me now when I reflect on the fact that it possibly became my single favourite moment from that whole period.

As the new line-up began to gel musically so in concert we started to develop a 'look'. It's interesting how what is often perceived as a conscious, studied, even manipulative image almost always has an innocent, often haphazard starting point. The 'Oxfam chic' thing that we had developed during those early years was purely an accident born of desperate dole-life penury but later seized upon by the editors of fashion magazines as some sort of style manifesto. Rather than it being a conscious decision, bands tend to dress similarly simply because they spend so much time with each other. Records are swapped and jackets are borrowed and minds become tuned to the same frequency and the flow of clothes like the flow of ideas is all part of that process. Of course this can be faked and manufactured by a Svengali-like manager and a clever stylist but I think you can always tell. A look often becomes an unwitting creation of both the band and the media and is tied up within the fabric of its persona in that it is something that is reflected back by journalists and incrementally and subconsciously fine-tuned. The *Coming Up* look was one of the few times that personally I think we got it right. When I come across press shots from other points in our career I cringe at how either we look like we've found the keys to our grandmother's dressing-up box or alternatively like we've been dressed by our mums to go to a wedding. For a band that is for some reason seen as being stylish I think we have sometimes had an embarrassing visual sense. I have often thought that the louche, vaguely sophisticated style that we found ourselves eventually inhabiting was actually paradoxically a factor of our working-class roots. Of course there will be many examples that seem to dis-prove this but within the demi-monde of alternative music I've noticed that there seems to be an inverse relationship between class and scruffiness, that it's those people who were born into comfortable homes, the children of middle-class professionals, who tend to dress down, probably to distance themselves from their backgrounds and to suggest a manufactured edge rather than one that is present. At the risk of coming across like an inverted snob myself I think those from working-class backgrounds who have been brought up wearing cheap supermarket clothes or stitched together hand-me-downs often feel the need to escape from the trappings of their humble origins, choosing, probably completely subconsciously, to suggest success in the clothes that they wear in the same way that the poorest families will often burden themselves with the cost of the most lavish weddings. To put it simply, poor people want to look rich and rich people want to look poor. This phenomenon has meant that often we have lurched between looking like we are trying too hard or looking like we haven't tried hard enough. The clothes we were wearing in 1996 seemed to sit on the right point along that spectrum. During an Asian tour I had managed to get a Portobello market seventies leather jacket copied by one of the many excellent Hong Kong tailors. In that carefree, easy way that bands have, as we began to spend more time together the style began to be borrowed by everyone and became a sort of unofficial uniform, like an embodiment of the music we were trying to make: something that was more an expression of the street, less precious and haughty and esoteric, something torn from the dirty pulse of the city, still romantic and passionate but tactile and very real. And as we all began to dress in a similar way so our lives became intertwined and we developed that secret language of camaraderie, an idiomatic landscape of in-jokes and impressions and shared understanding that only groups of people who have spent too much time together can acquire. There has always been a twisted, wry, dead-pan sense of humour in the Suede camp that has often gone unnoticed by the rest of the world, hidden as it is beneath a public veneer of perceived humourlessness. Mat and Richard especially are, in their own separate ways, two of the driest, wittiest people you are likely to meet and it was this shared lexicon that we began to develop as a band when Neil joined, filling the gaps I didn't know needed filling, realigning us and rebalancing us when I didn't realise we needed rebalancing. Although at first Neil very much politely slotted into the existing hierarchy, gradually as he revealed his strengths and gained confidence his role grew. I think for some people Neil's position in Suede, his purpose if you will, is still unclear. Even those who love the band will see an on-stage persona and assume that the studied laconic detachment that he projects somehow suggests that his role in the band is peripheral. Nothing could be further from the truth. As the years roll on and now we are faced with working on what will be our seventh album together Neil's role has never been more central, more vital. He is always challenging, always pushing me, always making me reach in and find the best in myself and without his presence Suede possibly might not have made it this far. The calumnious, now faintly hilarious, accusations of his being just 'indie eye candy' couldn't be more wrong as he increasingly reveals himself to be an artist of ever-growing stature. It's interesting to see how he has changed over the years. At first I think he was very conscious of fitting in around the existing power structure, sensitive to the dynamics of what made a guitar band function, realising of course that his position as a keyboard player was always going to be a somewhat fringe role and careful to not undermine or challenge that order. Incrementally and quite naturally though his role evolved and as he slowly gained confidence and experience the nuances and expertise of his musicianship became essential to us. These days his input in the studio especially is an absolutely key ingredient and without him we would be a completely different band, if we were indeed still a band at all. That might sound a little dramatic but it's his vision and sophisticated touch and tireless attention to detail that has allowed us to grow beyond the simplistic rock format as all bands must in order to survive, but in a manner that mirrors Richard's his public presence is almost demure, preferring as he does to just quietly and brilliantly get on with his work and leave all of the shouting and vulgar attention grabbing to me.

Back to 1995 though and one day Richard had wandered over to the frenetic chaos of my flat, braving the throngs of swaying, chattering gurners who still hadn't realised it was time to go home and clutching a new demo cassette in his hands. It was something he had called 'Dead Leg', part of a series of tracks with working titles including one called 'Chinese Burn' that had comically mined the theme of playground bullying. When approaching a new song I like to try to hurriedly write down my very first responses to it as sometimes these can be the most powerful, often containing something direct and instinctive, before it becomes too familiar and you begin to overthink it. Bearing this in mind I like to listen to it completely alone when I'm prepared and ready to respond and feeling that my synapses are firing. So Richard just stayed and we chatted a bit and drank tea with sour milk and once he'd shuffled off back through the scattering leaves and the dirty pavements of Notting Hill I finally found the time to retreat into my studio, close the eight-inch-thick sound-proofed door and slot the cassette into my Tascam. I was greeted with a brilliantly wiry riff, cyclical and nagging and querulous, a line that bored like a parasite into your head and refused to leave. Around it I began to weave a kind of stream-of-consciousness rant, a cut-and-paste shot-gun tirade that threw around almost random images torn from the pages of my notebooks: 'high on diesel and gasoline / psycho for drum machine / shaking their tits to the hits'. I felt that frisson of uncontrollable excitement when you know there's something really great almost within your grasp, thrilling to the complex blend of danger and melody which in the right proportions have always been the hall-mark of a good Suede song. As I worked on it the simple, dislocated narrative began to reveal itself: a fragmented sketch of the chaos of my and Alan's dissolute world set amongst the heaving ash-trays and the broken glass and the endless drifting days; an exploration of the squalor and the fractured half-lives but with a celebratory, joyous tone that somehow glorified our unhinged carnival of madness. It was I suppose partly born of my constant need to try to romanticise the grubby edges of my world, to resist the stuffy conventions of acceptability, throwing away the furtive vestiges of paranoia and fear and proudly saying, 'This is my life – deal with it'. In a move that paralleled the writing of 'Saturday Night' I found Richard's original chorus chords too complex so I re-wrote them as a very simple C/Em/F/G sequence and sang over it: 'Here they come, the beautiful scum, the beautiful scum'. I liked the idea of a twisted anthem for the anti-hero that the words suggested but on further reflection it seemed a little wayward and marginal so I changed the title to 'Beautiful Ones' and the song was born. Alan's party was still going on upstairs so after a few hours' work I wandered up to rejoin it, slotting in on the black L-shaped sofa and amongst the debris covering the glass-top table and we carried on into the next day and when everyone had finally left I excitedly played him the half-ideas on the messy, sketchy demo. Alan has always been such a passionate, supportive friend when it comes to my work and he immediately loved the song and in his rapacious, relentless way kept wanting to hear it again and again. Unfortunately my mediocre guitar-playing wasn't improved by my now completely frazzled state so we called Richard up and he trudged back over to North Kensington and stepped gingerly back into our scattered world, trying to readjust to the odd temporal shift – the displacement and chaos that must have seemed like a frozen moment from the previous day – and all crammed like sardines into my tiny, airless, orange studio he and I ran through the track, the sweat beading on our foreheads as Alan squatted on the floor smoking, a huge contented grin spreading across his handsome, ravaged face. Well, at least that's how I remember the genesis of the song. If you asked Richard to supply a version of the events his more sober memories might be less pithy and probably more accurate but as Mark Twain once so brilliantly said: 'Never let the truth get in the way of a good story'. The song was hard to get right in the studio as Richard went through endless guitar variations before he finally nailed the right sound for the all-important riff but eventually it would become possibly our most successful ever, a jagged, ragged anthem for the disaffected; one of those 'entry-level' tracks that many people who don't know much about the band are vaguely familiar with. I wouldn't say it's my personal favourite – it's almost too popular to deserve too much of my affection – but it's a song that has connected in such a way that it always makes the floor heave when we play it live and as such has become one of a small handful that we now simply don't have a choice but to perform at shows.

One day Neil wandered over to my house. At the time he was still living in his flat in Crouch End and had been beavering away on a demo for me. Because he didn't have any paper at home he had written the chords on the back of a Haringey Council Public Works notice which he'd torn from a lamp-post outside and wrapped around the cassette. Neil had titled the demo 'Tiswas' and it was a slippery, spidery, wriggling sort of neurotic guitar beast, punchy and direct but strangely complex and meandering too. I immediately loved it and one afternoon while Alan slumbered next door, recovering from our usual nightly carnival of excess, I went about writing a paean to the guileless beauty of pop fandom, a song detailing a young girl's nascent obsessions, her wild-eyed love for the mercurial wonders of the charts, and I called it 'Starcrazy'. Despite its capricious, often inane nature I've always had a fascination with the uncomplicated appeal of pop, how in an almost quasi-religious way it can fulfill and enlighten and complete people's lives and provide them with a strange kind of empowerment. I love its inherently democratic nature, its accessibility, the fact that unlike fine art or ballet it speaks to real people about their lives and is within everyone's grasp. I love that my copy of *The White Album* is exactly the same as Bill Gates'. It's a discipline that especially interested me while making this album: that chase for unembellished directness, that pursuit of the *mot juste*, that feeling that the simplest of lyrics could unlock something timeless and powerful and universal and that ultimate sense that it might be just within your grasp to whisper down through the generations.

IT SOUNDS LIKE THE
FUCKING SMURFS

As I stood on the up escalator at Holborn tube station
the tired huddle of rush-hour commuters being carried downwards stared blankly at us from across the
divide, any mild curiosity they might have felt as the
cameramen jostled into position around me negated
by a long day at work and by the numbing ubiquity
of such sights all over the streets of the capital. The
director slapped the hinged clap-stick on to the clap-
perboard and shouted, '*Action!*' and a swirl of distorted,
tinkling music flooded out of the portable monitors at
my feet like the demented accompaniment to a broken
fairground carousel. In order to chase a visual effect he
had insisted that the music be played at double time
and my cheeks stung with a creeping kind of humilia-
tion as I mimed along to the comical volley of sped-up
words realising with a writhing embarrassment that

I was sounding like I'd swallowed the contents of a helium balloon. Those on the down escalator swivelled their faces towards me, gazing in silent incredulity as I underwent my ordeal, their eyes locked on the spectacle, their brows knitted in amusement and mild confusion. Finally, thankfully, the music finished and all I could hear beyond the blood singing in my ears was the rumble of the escalators and the shuffle of feet. Suddenly, to my eternal shame, from within the anonymous throng a clear, mocking voice rang out against the mutter and hubbub: 'He sounds even more like the fucking Smurfs!'

We started work on the album at Townhouse Studios in Shepherd's Bush in autumn 1995. Even though we'd met with a couple of other producers to see what they had to say as soon as we got in a room with Ed again it just felt right. I think in many ways Ed was even more driven than the band at this point to make this album work; he had developed a burning zeal, a wild-eyed personal quest which meant that he had drifted beyond the normal boundaries of his job description into a kind of rapt obsession. Possibly his biggest motivation was that even though I don't think it had been mentioned in interviews at that point there were industry mutterings about Bernard having left the band through a dissatisfaction with Ed's work. Of course Chinese whispers like that could never reveal the rich complexity of the situation but they planted a malign seed that Ed understandably felt he must try to root out. This is one of the reasons that our relationship with him over the years has drifted beyond the limits of his remit with a wonderful almost familial sense of shared history which means that for him working with Suede is never just another job, and it was this hunger that drove through him and in turn bled into us and laid the bed-rock for the album sessions.

When making records it often feels that Suede is caught in a cycle of opposition against itself. Sometimes it feels that there is a pendulum that swings between creative poles defining the nature of the next album by inverting the qualities of the last. For many reasons, the swing between *Dog Man Star* and its successor felt like it had to be a bold, confident statement of intent, that the character of the new work should diametrically oppose that of the last. The fiery forge in which *Dog Man Star* had been birthed had been so uncomfortable and at times so unpleasant that we had all decided that we simply couldn't go back there and so we decided to make a pop album: 'just ten hits' was the wry mantra that we often used to describe the intention. We wanted the record to be everything that *Dog Man Star* wasn't – punchy, direct and bristling with hooks – something that reflected the language of the street, not some distant, aloof, esoteric, fantasy netherworld. Sometimes in a crazed desire to stick to this self-imposed dogma I think we pushed the songs too far along that spectrum, but when making an album I often find that you need, at least initially, rules and structures and guidelines to give the record form and consistency or it can be in danger of becoming a random murky soup of disconnected songs. And so with our mantra ringing in our ears we became slightly obsessed with trying to make almost every track sound like a single whether that suited their inherent feel or not. This was back in the days when there was still the media infrastructure for bands like ours to penetrate the mainstream as during the mid-nineties the mainstream had seemed to shift even further left field which, apart from its rejection of American cultural imperialism, was possibly the only other good thing about the guitar-based scene that was burgeoning so clamorously around us. We would attempt radically different versions of the songs, sometimes dressing them up in clothes that simply didn't suit them. Ed often supplied models of chart hits into which he thought he could twist our music, and he would hustle and harry us into rehearsing with this kind of style or that kind of attitude. One of these bonkers moments happened with 'She', which he thought he could make sound more like Edwyn Collins' 'A Girl Like You' and thus I suppose unlock more of its mainstream potential. This whole episode became rather a sticking point and though the friction it created between us now seems comical at the time

I remember throbbing with passive aggression as we sourly and reluctantly ran through a sped-up version of the song while Ed overdubbed some vibraphone ideas to try to drag it away from its grinding, rocky core and force it uncomfortably into some lighter, groovier, *Faux-town* black hole. Another of these bizarre ambitions that he had was for 'Filmstar' to sound more akin to the Babylon Zoo hit 'Spaceman' and so we spent many wasted, unenthusiastic hours trying to stretch the song and speed it up and give it a pop sheen that it simply didn't suit. To be fair Ed was just experimenting and when it became blindingly obvious that the songs worked much better as dark, prowling rock beasts he held up his hands and we went back to the original ideas. With the beauty of hindsight it's easy to laugh at the mistakes you make and the cul-de-sacs you go down but sometimes this kind of lateral thinking when making music can pay off, taking a song to places that no one knew it could go, stretching it and releasing something within it that you didn't know was there. 'Beautiful Ones' was less contentious in that it was already a catchy pop number but Ed and Richard spent countless days throwing different guitar sounds at the riff, trying to find *the* sound that suited the knotty, nagging infectious hook. During the course of this Odyssey they even recorded a steel-bodied Dobro resonator guitar used more in traditional blues music and at some point the riff was even heavily phased giving the whole intro a horrible gimmicky sixties feel. Eventually the part was comprised of an amalgam of sounds, a blend of Jaguars and 335s and Telecasters, but the journey to reach that point was onerous and winding and inevitably cyclical. I think Ed saw that with Bernard now gone his role within the power structure of the band had changed. He realised that he had much more creative freedom to experiment and mould. Previously Bernard's musical direction had been visionary and commanding and bordering on dictatorial and I don't mean that as a criticism. It's incredibly important that there is a single strong voice or sometimes a pair of voices when making records. Albums that are made by committee are doomed to sound like a grey mesh of disconnected ideas; a band needs a leader and a focal point just as much as any connected group of people and Bernard's voice was always the strongest and most heard when it came to these matters. I have always needed a musical foil to bounce my scruffy, sketchy half-ideas against and have technically never been a good enough musician to completely take control of the reins in the studio, so sensing that the role was now vacated I think Ed began to fill a different, less passive space, not in any sinister autocratic sort of way but simply because the dynamics had changed and with Neil and Richard still as yet vastly inexperienced the whole project needed a firm, guiding hand.

During my snatched hours away from the labyrinth of the studio I had started to pay visits to the designer Peter Saville with whom I was developing sleeve ideas. Like countless other young men in countless other bedrooms I had sat there as a teenager gazing into the abstract, unreadable enigma that was the cover to *Unknown Pleasures* so when Saul had cleverly suggested him and had arranged for us to meet at the Nude offices it felt that somehow a part of the fabric of my childhood was about to come to life. Peter is without doubt one of my favourite people in the music business. He is a rare flower of wit and sophistication in a barren desert of desperate ill-mannered bullies. At the time he was living in Mayfair rather like a character from an Evelyn Waugh novel in a hilarious parody of a wealthy playboy's pad. After ascending in one of those ancient, caged Edwardian lifts you would be greeted at the door by his assistant and led into the flat and offered a seat on a Mies Van Der Rohe Barcelona chair or a similarly designed piece of elegant modern furniture formed of leather and brushed steel. The apartment was rich with thick, seventies shag-pile rugs and pop-art paintings and expensive-looking textiles and everywhere were scattered fine art and photography books. After half an hour or so of flicking through images of scantily clad women a real scantily clad woman would sometimes waft through the spacious lounge with bed-hair, smoking and muttering something into the phone in a German accent and eventually Peter would descend like some bleary-eyed aristocrat in his customary silk dressing gown yawning his apologies and asking for coffee. We would then spend shifting, merging hours just talking. Peter is one of those people with whom the conversation spools and fragments, drifting off ever more into tangents as, fascinated and fascinating, he navigates the channels of his meandering thought. Eventually the subject would settle on the matter in hand and we would finally focus on our ideas for the sleeve artwork. In amongst his huge stockpile of books we had found one by a German artist called Paul Wunderlich and loved the charged, surreal depictions of warped sexuality. They hinted at a kind of pop-art sensibility but with their own distinctive mien: stylised and taut with suggestion and beautifully strange. We decided to use them as our guide for the look of the sleeve. Peter was convinced that we could manipulate a photograph to imbue it with the same feel and so we went about staging something using models to create a kind of human tableau that paralleled some of the dissolute themes of the record. Peter's friend Nick Knight took some beautiful photographs and the resulting sleeve opened a new visual lexicon for us and was the birth of a friendship between Peter and myself that has spanned decades.

Back in the real-world grey of the studio Ed's

enthusiasm to make everything sound upbeat had even extended to the ballads and I wandered in one day to lay down my vocal to 'Saturday Night' to find that the backing track had been recorded much too fast so when faced with the task of singing I was simply unable to fit in the words. Unfortunately when I listened back it felt hurried and crammed and mechanical and bereft of charm, lacking any of the poetry that good phrasing can lend a lyric. We eventually ended up slowing it down and getting the speed of the track more or less right but I always feel that a song has a natural tempo that it's the band's job to find. As a singer my instinct probably veers towards a slower pace, feeling that somehow it unlocks a heft and a size to the music, that it gives the space that allows me to deliver the narrative properly and to lend the song lilt and ebb. Ed on the other hand was convinced that everything had to be faster, that the true pop heart of the album could only be unlocked with punch and haste and brevity. It was a struggle between us that inevitably led to an imbalance as we pulled in different directions and started to mistrust each other, him wanting one thing and me childishly contradicting him and demanding the opposite. It was responsible for one of my biggest regrets concerning that album – the vari-speed vocals. In the days before the digital wonders of Logic and Pro-Tools when everything was recorded on to two-inch tape the only way you could change the speed of a track was to slow the tape down or speed it up but this of course resulted in a subtle change in pitch. We had used vari-speeding before on things like 'Metal Mickey'; it was a well-known technique that, if used subtly, could somehow nicely glue the sonic components of the track together, and if you listen carefully you can hear it on a whole galaxy of well-known pop songs from the pre-digital age, from The Beatles to Abba, but without a careful, stayed hand it can make the singer sound like Mickey Mouse. When we got to the mixing stage it was deemed by those in charge of the more technical aspects of the record that some of the songs were too slow and would benefit from radical vari-speeding. Looking back I think it's a shame that I didn't stand firm and trust my instincts but by that point I was caught up in a scrabbling, undignified chase for success, seeing the prize dangling before me and believing that the only way to grasp it would be to ignore the nagging voices inside. Many songs that shouldn't have underwent this pitch-control technique which I feel gives parts of the album a lightly mechanised, slightly artificial sheen. Perhaps that suits some of the deliberately blithe, disposable themes like those in 'Beautiful Ones' and 'Filmstar', but I also like to flatter myself that in many of the tracks there's a soul and a grace that it betrays. Our single biggest mistake in this respect though was how one song in particular ended up sounding. It was towards the end of the sessions when Saul started muttering about how he didn't think we yet had the first single. An A&R man's role is a strange, unenviable one. It's his job to be dissenting and questioning at times, to push and demand, to be unpopular and to force the band to stretch themselves. Often though, as they are kept to a certain extent at arms' length from the creative hub, theirs is a frustrating task; knowing what they want but lacking the expertise to be able to explain it or sometimes the access to be able to influence anyone. Again, like Ed, it always felt that Saul had a very personal relationship with Suede, that he cared about us beyond a point that was professional and that his life was deeply meshed with ours. It was I suppose something that we had fostered and encouraged and which lent our whole set-up a strong sense of family, a feeling that our fortunes were locked together 'for better or for worse' and that as with any family there were inevitable quarrels and spats and sulks but you walked away and forgot them and moved on, your bonds somehow strengthened through the trials of your vicissitudes and mutual experience. Saul knew as well as any of us that the album had to be a bullet-proof comeback or we would suffer fatal wounds from the circling predators of the press who had smelled blood and begun to move in for the kill and he felt that we should summon our strength and push ourselves to write one defining song which would act as a figure-head for the campaign.

In the early summer Richard had given me a demo that he had jokingly called 'Pisspot'. To be honest I can't even remember what it sounded like now because the song ended up undergoing so many changes as to be unrecognisable from the one on the original cassette that had littered the MDF shelves of my scruffy little orange studio back in Chesterton Road. I must have liked something about it but asked Richard to change the chorus and so he delivered a beautiful sweeping chord sequence, lyrical and flowing and suggestive of something romantic and yearning over which for some reason I decided to write a tawdry fiction about being confronted by pictures of an ex-girlfriend in a pornographic magazine. It was a jarring mismatch so I tore up that idea and raided my notebooks and came up with a new one, this time singing, 'Oh, oh, oh, you and me, we're the litter on the breeze, we're the lovers on the streets' over the chords. It was an incredibly thrilling moment; there was a grace and a poetry to the melody and the words which I loved but I felt now that the verse was wrong. Sensing that something special was almost in our grasp for many weeks we threw ideas at it until one day in the studio I was strumming and humming away in that slightly irritating, distracting way that people in control rooms do when I hit upon a simple C/Em/F/D/G sequence which Ed, brimming with the kind of wild-eyed enthusiasm that makes him so great to work with, absolutely adored and the chords and melody were nailed. I went home and worked on the lyrics, writing a kind of romantic, generic street anthem, something that borrowed the 'us against the world' sentiment of 'Hand In Glove' or 'Heroes' and I called it 'Trash': a song which both accepted and celebrated the drab, limiting world of my humble beginnings, a song about love and poverty and class and one which ended up introducing the album to the world. 'Trash' was always so important for me and I think in a wider sense for the band itself. Apart from it being a very successful comeback single that silenced many doubters and muted many naysayers it was written as a kind of 'band anthem'. It was a song which attempted to detail, I admit somewhat romantically, the characteristics of the members of the band – our collective identity – and in a broader sense I think that of our fans. It must have been inspired by the very tribalistic, playground pop culture of warring gangs that I grew up with whereby you defined yourself as a person by the music you listened to and wore your passion like a badge of honour, something for which you would often be willing to suffer. In many ways I think 'Trash' was my attempt to describe and in some ways manufacture a 'tribe' for myself; to plot points on a cultural graph that I and people like me could inhabit. My strange upbringing with a Liszt-obsessed taxi driver in a council house full of Aubrey Beardsley prints had marinaded me wonderfully within a

curious soup of dissonant ingredients but it had ultimately left me with a sense of never quite belonging;
too poor to be accepted by the middle class to which my
parents' values covertly aspired but too different to fit
in to the working-class community in which we lived
which viewed us somewhat suspiciously as distant and
aloof. I had always slightly envied those Manchester
bands for whom their 'people' were already waiting, lying dormant, ready to be activated should the
moment come, but for Suede I think ours were much
less regional but still out there somewhere and 'Trash'
was my attempt to find them. I had been searching for
a while and all of those early songs that had tried to
establish a collective identity were hinting at it – 'We
Are The Pigs', 'The Wild Ones' and even things like
'So Young' were all attempts at locating an army, a
herd, a gang of people who felt the same as me – but
'Trash' was much more explicit, providing a kind of
manifesto of what it meant to be a 'Suede person'.
For Richard particularly the song was an especially
important moment which marked his transition from
a talented copyist into a fine writer, finally emerging
from Bernard's smothering shadow and being accepted
and loved by the fans as an artist in his own right.

Inspired by spending drifting, bleary mornings-after
staring at *Sky News* trailers I called the album *Coming
Up*, liking the way it suggested a sense of anticipation
and an unembellished simplicity but also very aware

of the colloquial meaning of the phrase – the sly, idiomatic implication of chemical rush and elation – thrilling again, as with my mischievous lyrics for 'Animal Nitrate', at the thought that I might be able to smuggle something vaguely poisonous into the fortress of the mainstream.

GO TO HIS HOUSE
AND KILL HIS CAT

As I picked my way along Chesterton Road my eyes flitted casually over the usual scatter of empty cans and heaving binbags and dog shit that littered the kerb. In the road there was a new bit of graffiti which I hadn't previously noticed but I was late and the words were facing the wrong way so I didn't bother reading it. As I got closer to my flat though I saw that the same person had scrawled something in the same white paint on the pavement just by the house. The words formed slowly with every step I took until at last I saw the whole thing stark and plain against the grey concrete: *BRETT ANDERSON LIVES AT NUMBER 106 CHESTERTON ROAD. GO TO HIS HOUSE AND KILL HIS CAT.*

Long studio sessions can make you feel like you are

losing yourself in some dark windowless maze. Endless drifting hours are spent in closed, hermetically sealed air-conditioned rooms where the lack of natural light confuses your circadian rhythms and the emotional intensity and the physical challenge can push you to the thresholds of your endurance. A strange kind of bunker mentality can develop whereby you begin to experience mild Stockholm syndrome: an unhealthy surrender to the conditions of your willing imprisonment and the team of people that you are with become as familiar as close family. It's a charged crucible, an arena that can sometimes break bands and sometimes strengthen their bonds as they all push in their own personal way towards the same goal – that of making a great record. The problem is that each of you has a slightly different definition of what a great record is and that differential can merge into disagreement. The minor conflicts and clashes that we had while making *Coming Up* were nothing unusual, just a necessary part of that process, the push and the pull and the struggle that should always accompany any creative endeavour – it's a sign that everyone involved cares and therefore its absence would actually be somewhat worrying. When cabs were called late into the night and we blearily made our way back home we were always able to leave our niggles at the door, never again allowing the issues to fester and decay and become wounding and personal. Possibly we had learned something from the fractious clashes while making *Dog Man Star* . . . although probably not. Despite my reservations about some aspects of the record I have to say I'm incredibly proud of *Coming Up*: it redefined what the band were and introduced us to a whole new audience and in many ways, given the challenge, it was a remarkable feat. I think it's important to not gloss over the frictions that strew the path though as somehow they make it more real and in the end it is often the story of these conflicts that is the interesting, most revealing part.

I sometimes reflect on the qualities that in my case have allowed me the luxury of living a life being paid for what I love doing the most. To be honest I'm not an especially naturally talented musician nor an artistic visionary nor even a particularly gifted storyteller. One characteristic that has helped me over the years though is the fact that I simply never give up. I'm aware that it's a trait that doesn't fit with the romantic notion of the enigmatic artist but this book isn't about perpetuating those fictions and it's an attribute that anyone who wants to get anywhere needs to acquire. In my case it has been something born from a mixture of incommensurate, hubristic self-belief and a desperate fear of poverty and has meant that after every seismic career crisis I have somehow found the energy to pick myself up and dust myself off and start again. And so, against all the odds, like in some hackneyed film about a plucky misunderstood underdog we had clawed our way back. Maligned, written-off and tarred and feathered by the press we had returned to the fray, scrapping and resilient: 'the battle-scarred fighters who just won't go down'. We released 'Trash' and then *Coming Up* in the late summer of 1996 to rapturous excitement and acclaim, the album hurtling to number one and going gold and platinum in many corners of Europe, and then embarked on an eighteen-month campaign of touring taking us in endless circling loops around Europe and Asia: rattling, swaying expeditions on countless tour buses and through numberless airports and an infinity of sound checks and blank backstage dressing rooms laden with mini-fridges and cheese platters until disorientated and unwashed we would be deposited like worn-out luggage back in London and make our unsteady way back to our homes to try to pick up some semblance of normality. I suppose this is probably the time for me to regale you with stories of on-tour japery and excess, the florid cartoon life of a band that those on the outside assume is being conducted by those on the road: the Dionysian sagas of glut and madness and bad behaviour, the misogynistic *Loaded*-style laddish cavalcade of 'birds and booze' and frenzied overindulgence. Strangely though I find it hard to remember touring in any detail, and what detail I can remember just fits in with the clichés that everyone would expect: the predictable dreary blur of alcohol and narcotics and dalliances with kitten-eyed foreign women. I tend to switch my mind to quite an animalistic setting while touring, my focus narrowing down to the simple requirements of sleep and food and intemperance. Of course there have been colourful incidents – waking up in a drunken stupor on the floor of a public toilet in Stockholm to the flashing bulbs of the paparazzi, having coins thrown at me on stage by packs of angry thugs in Cologne, Jägermeister-fuelled evenings with random eighties popstars in Oslo – but recounting them in any detail beyond a brief mention leaves this book in danger of becoming just another wave in the sea of stories detailing the same predict-able rat-run of jolly schoolboy-like shenanigans that allegedly all bands get up to and I promised myself that I would never write that kind of thing. In many ways such anecdotes seem somehow tangential to the tale that I am trying to tell. I want this to be less of a list of 'stuff that's happened to me' and more of an investigation into other events and their consequences and so despite their graphic nature these kind of travel stories are in many ways peripheral. The only interesting thing that I can think of to mention about touring is how numbing it is. I've always found the whole experience so incredibly physically demanding that my intellect and creativity become secondary in order to indulge the tyrant of my body. Rather like when I'm on a long-haul flight and find that I am only able to watch the kind of 'comfort viewing' that

I would never consider in my everyday life so I feel that my IQ levels drop dramatically when I'm on tour. Therefore we've never been one of those bands who have been able to write on the road, unable to indulge in that trope of the bearded, weary musicians gathered in a dishevelled hotel suite jamming away on their acoustic guitars while bleary-eyed waifs sit smoking and nodding along in the corner. Apart from the odd phrase or lyric smuggled into the ever-present bank of my notebooks the creative process gets put on hold. In many ways I quite like how this enforced abstinence dictates a kind of rhythm to the whole artistic cycle, allowing me to rest my mind for a while and let my subconscious do some work. I always imagine this process to be a little like how in agriculture a farmer will allow a field to become fallow for a while in order that it can be more productive in the future. The only song in our back catalogue that I think has been directly inspired by touring was called 'Have You Ever Been This Low?', a bleak, smeary sketch of the tedious drudgery of the experience that I penned hunched over my cream cheese bagel and my bottle of Snapple in a diner somewhere in Boston on the *Dog Man Star* tour. Slightly tangentially, the role of the subconscious is a fascinating thing when it comes to writing. Often when wrestling with the conundrum of a lyric or a melody I will take a break and go for a walk and forget about the problem for a while and let my mind settle only to return to my work and find that magically the *mot juste* has sprung into my head, my subconscious having been chipping away while I've been wandering around staring at some sparrows. It doesn't always happen but when it does it feels like a wonderful gift and has resulted in so many crucial little snippets of our songs all the way from the 'you're taking me over' hook of 'The Drowners' to the chorus of 'Cold Hands' and many, many things in between.

Back to the story though and by this juncture in our careers a legal dispute with an American lounge singer called Suede had forced us to change our name in that country. It was a rather sorry episode and happened at a point when our lives had accelerated to such a strange place that our judgement was utterly skewed by the carnival of madness and we somehow allowed ourselves to become known in that country as The London Suede – *Suede, London* being what was stencilled all over our flight cases. The clunky ugliness of the moniker was possibly the defining reason why beyond that event we tended to avoid playing in the States, unable to face the ignominy of touring under such a humiliatingly silly name. The British media would often go on to frame our relative failure in America as due to our overt 'Englishness', choosing to portray us as a reaction to grunge and assuming that the idiosyncrasies of my character in particular were diametrically opposed to those values and couldn't possibly fit within that market. In reality I had no problem with grunge – at least it seemed to possess a rage and an energy and I think in many ways its best moments still resonate – and I loved playing shows in the States, many of which were riotous and exciting. Sadly it wasn't to be but it was a course of events that led us to embrace touring in parts of the world that we might never have bothered with and focusing instead on working Europe and Asia with an energy that might have been otherwise unavailable to us. We played huge, rowdy, passionate shows everywhere from Copenhagen to Singapore as the seemingly endless procession rolled on and on. It's a strange, dislocating experience returning from lengthy tours. The regular, bestial rituals that you undergo every night and the forced intimacy of life on the road are suddenly replaced with relative calm and stasis and propriety. The complex tapestry of in-jokes and shared private references, despite being the only language that you become able to communicate in, is suddenly bereft of context leaving you sometimes with a feeling of being stranded and unheard: unable to fit back in, squirming and restless and disconnected. It was in this state that I would shakily make my way back to Chesterton Road every few months often to find that the unsettled disorder in which I had left the flat was completely unchanged, like a finger had pressed pause on some celestial tape deck. Alan was

still locked within the same scurrying, hedonistic ceremonies, the same bluish smoke filled the same rooms,
the same thin patina of cigarette ash was everywhere,
the dead flowers were browner, the matted floors
more scattered, the LPs more scratched and the same
heaving bins were still waiting to be taken out. The
mainstream success of the record had begun to attract
a regular smattering of fans who would sometimes
congregate in sorry huddled groups on the pavement
below. Despite making me a little uncomfortable I
would always try to be polite and dispose myself to
their small litany of requests but once I remember
sitting upstairs in the flat with Alan and Sam after a
particularly gruelling session and being bombarded
throughout the mid-morning by a relentless nagging
barrage of intercom buzzes so that Sam, her patience
having finally deserted her and bristling with an
uncharacteristic irritation, marched angrily to the
kitchen and filled a pan with cold water, tipping it over
the balcony on to the pavement below like a knight
throwing oil over the battlements of a castle during a
medieval siege. The resulting incredulous shrieks from
four floors below made us all feel rather guilty but at
least we were left in peace for a while. Another time I
was trotting along Chesterton Road on my way back
to the flat when I bumped into a couple of European
fans and in my uncomfortable, inelegant rush to get
away from them stupidly said something like, 'But

I'll be back in a couple of days – come back then,' not realising of course that what I had intended as a polite wriggle out of the situation would be interpreted as a formal invitation. It was a misunderstanding born of my social anxiety and increasing inability to deal with the customs and conventions of the real world, something that was being finely tuned by still growing levels of success and excess. Unfortunately I believe that it led to an unpleasant campaign of abuse against me when those in question returned at the appointed time to be confronted with my inevitable absence and in their impotent rage took it upon themselves to graffiti the pavements and parts of the surrounding streets with my name and address and deeply disturbing threats. It inspired a song at the time called 'Graffiti Women' and it was a glimpse into the shadowy margins of fandom, the tenebrous hinterland where attractions become obsessions which in turn become nefarious compulsions. In a way I think it's tied up with the person versus persona question – how when meeting their heroes fans are in a strange situation of meeting both the person and the persona at the same time and that sometimes this disparity can throw up confusions and incongruities for them as they struggle between the perfect image that they have and the real person with whom they are confronted who in many ways is always bound to disappoint. Somehow this all felt far more threatening and darker than it probably was; possibly my growing paranoia and increasingly neurotic disposition exaggerated the whole thing but it marked the end of a chapter for me, providing a turning point and an impetus to move on.

We left the flat in a chaotic flurry one night, the bemused removal men trying to pick their way around the madness of the permanent party which our lives had become, packing and carrying out boxes while we sat like lords in our ash-scattered kingdom of debris, lost in a hedonistic solipsism, oblivious to the scurrying world beyond ourselves. We were carried aloft and bundled into vans, our tatty, unmended possessions thrown roughly into cardboard boxes and the cargo dumped unceremoniously at what was to become our new home – a ground-floor flat on the corner of Ledbury and Artesian Road. It was an elegantly corniced, high-ceilinged Victorian conversion with a spacious, bright, west-facing lounge that looked out on to the bustling street. What I didn't know until I moved there was how much I had missed that little enclave. The flat was two streets away from Moorhouse Road and our old flat which had been the charmed and tatty stage that had spewed forth so many ideas for the debut album. I've always had an affinity for that part of town – its unassuming, quiet elegance, its anti-dote to the wedding-cake showiness of those grander houses further west. I filled the flat with lilies and found shadowy, fabric pop-art portraits to hang above the mantelpiece, enjoying again living within a more ornamental, less characterless space. Looking back, this was a golden time for me. Sometimes these periods only reveal themselves with hindsight, the jostle of the day-to-day obscuring their true worth, but if there is a real state called happiness then it was around this time that I was again finally feeling my way back towards its fleeting, shifting borders with a sense of having weathered a leaden storm and of having emerged on calmer, brighter seas.

One day though I was pottering around arranging ornaments and humming to myself when the phone rang. 'Hi Brett,' drawled a familiar voice, 'it's Justine'.

PART FOUR

QUIET RUIN

A scruffy, shuffling man made his way down the street, his sickle-bent body hunched against the bitter slap of the wind, the threadbare, black Oakland Raiders baseball cap pulled tightly over his unwashed hair shadowing his deadened, downcast petrol-blue eyes as they flickered over the dirty pavement tracking the ballet of the scattering litter and hiding his ashen face and waxy skin from anyone who might chance to glance his way. Clutching one hand against his neck to gather his tatty black coat further in against the cold, he held in his other a blue plastic corner-shop bag containing his usual small list of seemingly random purchases – Blu-Tack, straws, kitchen foil, elastic bands, household ammonia and a small bottle of Mars Bar drink – a collection of apparently perfectly innocent everyday objects but which to those in the know combine to take on an unwholesome, troubling, very specific meaning.

Fishing into the jumbled mess of his pockets he found his keys and with a trembling hand fitted them into the Yale lock and pushed open the front door of his home. Even though it was midday the curtains were still pulled together, screening the flat from the street and obscuring the view of the old Victorian red-brick wall opposite which hid the houses of Westbourne Park Villas from the high-speed trains which clattered and rumbled and whooshed as they pulled away from Paddington Station. The door opened on to a large basement lounge area, its polished wooden floors a sea of scattered CDs and chipped wine-stained glasses and unemptied ash-trays, broken lighters and empty cat-food tins and Rizlas and empty cigarette packets; an untidy tangle of disorder, a small wasteland of cluttered domestic chaos. In the corner of the room the television rambled on quietly to itself, usually a daytime talk show that no one was listening to or muted images of saucer-eyed nubile dancers gyrating to MTV hits. Gathered around the glass-top table was a small collection of random, derelict, spent-looking people all lost in their own private shame as they tried to hide their greed behind fragments of fractured half-conversation, their darting eyes awaiting the hit that would send them back to their world of temporary calm. The days would melt into nights and the nights back into days again and the same sorry cast would still be sat in the same spots performing the same degrading ritual in a hellish circling loop until eventually the source of their mania would run out and they would be forced to leave or navigate a path that slalomed the sharp corners of the real world in order to seek out more of the stuff. And then it would begin again.

This was the awful trough into which my and Alan and Sam's lives had slumped, the pit of turpitude, the slithering bowels of shame. In one of the grand, empty, high-ceilinged master bedrooms upstairs the bare floorboards were painted black and the ornate windows gazed south beyond the wrought-iron balcony and over an increasingly riotous untended eighty-foot garden which was slowly reclaiming the soil so carefully tilled by the previous owner. At the foot of the garden there sat a gorgeous little summer house, probably once loved and looked after and filled with laughing children and frolicking pets but now just a bleak extension to our barren world of barely functioning addiction, a litter of empty bottles and cigarette ash and the debris of used paraphernalia. When it finally grabs hold of you like that there's no longer anything vaguely fun or sociable about the experience. Your goals in life become narrowed down to one simple quest: a base, animalistic drive to chase the one thing that will make you feel normal again, the one thing that makes you feel anything. Our lives had slowly slipped into this sorry slurry in a boringly pre-dictable, invidious, incremental march: the substances becoming slowly harder, the evenings becoming slowly more humourless, the chances of escape from it all slowly less likely. Of course I will now often reflect on the reasons that I seemed happy to be so blasé with my life and career. It's easy to want to blame some sort of shortcoming in your childhood, some perceived emotional injustice or lack of parental love or something else of which you think you may have been deprived but the truth was that despite the usual shadows and spectres that lurk on the fringes of any kid's psyche my childhood was remarkably content. Sure I developed neurosis and paranoia and anxieties but nothing happened that I would describe as trauma, nothing that I could point to accusingly and say, 'That's the reason!' No, looking back, my entry point into the whole pitiful arena I think I have to shamefully but honestly admit was just a simple quest for romantic escape, a longing to wander the same strange transgressive paths as Aldous Huxley or John Lennon, to walk hand in hand with Aleister Crowley or Thomas De Quincy; a frustrated suburban boy's search for the glamour of the outré, a reality beyond the grey, twee, suffocating lives that I saw being lived all around me as a young man. Of course I think I viewed my continuing success as a musician as something that gave me a licence to keep experimenting, to keep pushing the boundaries of respectability and when the little voices would whisper their disquiet into my ears during the cold, friendless hours just before dawn I would silence them by justifying my journey of abuse as a moral imperative of my position as an artist, as a kind of requirement of the job. While making *Coming Up* I had managed the balance successfully, keeping enough distance from the grubby clutches of that world to be able to retreat and observe and portray it. It was an immersion but one over which I still had control. As 1997 melted into 1998 though I was introduced to new, increasingly dangerous playmates who would command a different more consuming fealty and I began to be dragged into its sordid pit, a place from which no one gets out unscathed. The fun and levity that used to surround my and Alan's evenings had blown away like the white smoke that we pushed out of our lungs as we took on a dulled, functional approach to the proceedings; ours a mechanised need, a hungry graceless chase void of humour or love or even of any real enjoyment.

I'm not sure whether the rest of the band was aware of what was happening to me. My understanding of the world was ever narrowing to the epicentre of the glass-topped table around which my friends and I permanently perched as we conducted our obsessive new duties like devout acolytes attending to a shrine. After having finally all staggered off the bus for the last time at the end of the crushing eighteen-month world tour I think all the members of the band desperately needed space from each other away from the cloying, smothering intimacy that life on the road forces upon you. And so we had become consciously atomised, pottering around the meandering paths of our private lives, knowing that at some point the need to work would resurface, but for now content to let the beast stay slumbering in the murky depths. Justine had ambled back into my life. The years of estrangement and distance had muted the jagged, raw edges of my feelings towards her and I was able to welcome her back more as a long-lost friend than an errant lover and we began to get to know each other all over again but in a different, more decorous way. I think our mutual success had shifted the dynamic between us and forced us to communicate as different people cast in different roles, the former tensions and memories and betrayals somehow seeming to have happened to somebody else. She was in the lonely death throes of a dying relation-ship and I felt like I had personally evolved beyond the need to be sour or recriminating and so we wandered around the sun-kissed streets of Notting Hill together in the pulsing summer of 1997, buying bric-a brac and drinking coffee in the same sort of easy, untethered way that we had when we first met at university back in the eighties. The summer had culminated in a very public reconciliation when she had jumped on stage with Suede during our headline slot at Reading Festival and we had squawked along together excitedly to a scrappy version of an old song we had once jokingly written as a Fall parody called 'Implement, Yeah'. I was looking for somewhere new to live as the flat in Ledbury Road was just too small so we had browsed a few estate agents' windows and eventually found what seemed through the flattering lens of summer to be a beautiful maisonette in Westbourne Park Villas. In my studiedly insouciant way I had pretty much agreed to buy it there and then without paying much attention to, amongst other things, the mainline railway that rumbled a few metres away, but once I had moved in and the summer had browned into autumn and then the autumn had scattered into winter the flat had become darkened and stained by the increasingly poisonous routines of addiction as it slowly evolved into a kind of joyless, unloved stage upon which Alan and Sam and myself played out our shameful drama. There was something isolated about the place which perhaps allowed us the freedom to drift further away from the fringes of restraint. As it was on the edge of a train line there were no houses facing the entrance and the south side of the property backed on to the long garden which bordered someone else's equally long garden meaning that the next houses along on Westbourne Park Road stretched so far away from us as to be distant and inconsequential lending the whole maisonette a dislocated, unobserved kind of air – very unusual in London – like you were somehow removed from the normal rules of social cohesion that cheek-by-jowl city living requires. This rare peripheral quality meant that our routines felt completely unpoliced and unjudged and as by this point I had allowed myself to merge into another strange persona I managed to justify my ever more slanted, off-kilter life as an extension of my work. I suppose I'd always had this approach to my life; for years I'd seen my own personal happiness as secondary to the importance of the songs I was writing and I would often view it as just a vehicle that provided the raw fuel of subject matter, allowing myself to become exposed to increasingly bizarre and unlikely situations and fleeting, odd relationships in order that my songs breathed with a kind of truth. But that was when I was still in control. By the time I had moved into Westbourne Park Villas my priorities were shifting and my work was slowly becoming cuckolded as I began a passionate, doomed affair with the prickly mistress of my addiction.

Looking back at my life I have noticed an unusual dynamic that accompanies my work. It seems that I am always at my best when I have a point to prove or a challenge to overcome. The first album emerged from my struggle as a poor, timorous, suburban wannabe, *Dog Man Star* was born from the white-hot crucible of madness and conflict and success that the debut had propagated and *Coming Up* had been an album snatched against the odds from the savage jaws of failure. By the time we reached the fourth album however we had acquired a certain career stability, finding ourselves at a point where we felt less at odds and possibly more welcomed by the industry than ever. It was to be an illusion though and one which I think I subconsciously reacted to with an attitude of anti-careerist self-sabotage, finding in it instead of warmth and satisfaction a feeling of unpleasant smugness and of not belonging. I've always hated the self-serving, self-congratulatory closed circle of the industry and I have always strongly believed that the most interesting, vital voices are those on its outskirts away from the neutering forces of the red carpets and the awards ceremonies. Perhaps I'm just trying to intellectualise and justify my own weaknesses but as I felt us becoming ever more invited and accepted I think I subconsciously baulked and looked around for a spanner to plunge into the gears. And boy did I find one.

THE LITTLE OLD BEETLE
GOES ROUND AND ROUND
UNTIL HE ENDS UP RIGHT
UP TIGHT TO THE NAIL

The flat, endless summer sky stretched across London as little wispy white clouds gathered above the gardens behind Westbourne Park Villas. The whole enclave south of the railway line was ringing to the juddering, jarring rhythms of my inexpertly programmed Alesis SR16, the bass drum in the 'wrong' place, the tom where the kick should be, no hi-hat and always the only simple, childish grooveless patterns I could manage of beat/double beat. I twisted angrily at the controls of my Juno 106, looking for some sort of string sound and played a simple, one-fingered part against the pulse of the rhythm track, turning up the volume dial of the amplifier until the sound began to fracture. As I fumbled away frowning faces would peer quizzically out of windows wondering what could be making this unpleasant cacophony but, seeing nothing much beyond apart from the apple trees and the brambles, would disappear back into their homes grumbling and disturbed, unable to address their disquiet. If they had been able to glimpse beyond the rambling flora and into the flimsy wood and plate-glass summer house at the bottom of my untidy garden they would have witnessed a ravaged-looking spectre of a man, unwashed and unshaven and hollow-eyed crouched over the controls of his eight-track portastudio jamming in DATS and stabbing at buttons in a blind, frustrated, pointlessly aggressive attempt to master its mysteries. Summer houses being what they are there was very little in the way of either sound or heat insulation and so the occasional silences were smeared with the soft whoosh of a fan convection heater which when working would make the room too stuffy and when not would leave it gripped with a perishing chill. Apart from a bank of audio equipment and a few acoustic guitars and keyboards the place was still strewn with debris and paraphernalia, my notebooks jostling symbolically for space with torn Rizla packets and broken lighters and bits of burnt tin foil, and equally symbolically often finding no room and being abandoned to the cold-tiled floor, their sorry pages fluttering in the artificial breeze from the fan heater. I had developed a fairly quixotic vision of myself as the sort of musician who could write modern-sounding rock-based electronica. I think it was very much Justine's continuing influence due to her re-emergence into my life; she was introducing me to things like ESG and Faust, giving me a new direction in which I could see Suede travelling – somewhere starker and more contemporary and less oblique – a less poetic, veiled vision and I suppose one which frankly involved fewer guitars. This would of course inevitably lead to issues but let's sup with that problem later.

By this point in my career I think that my ego was, to say the least, burgeoning. The success of *Coming Up* and the circumstances in which we had beaten the odds had allowed me to weave a mythical web of indestructibility around myself. I had developed an illusion that there was very little I could do to avoid success and therefore a sudden veering off into addiction or teaching myself to write music in a completely alien way just seemed like diverting points on a path to continued good fortune. Also by this point in my life I had earned rather a lot of money, an obscene amount to be honest – an eye-watering figure from having re-signed a publishing deal after the success of *Coming Up* and its consequential tide of industry goodwill. I would normally shy away from brandishing showy facts like this but it seems to me that this windfall was one of the factors that led to my disintegration and so is an important step on the path of this tale.

After a childhood roaming the tatty fringes of penury and years of privation and threadbare insolvency as a young man I suddenly found myself not having to worry about money. If you have the good fortune to be used to that state then I'm sure it doesn't present too many problems but to someone like me, still with the faint waft of a Haywards Heath council estate on their person, it caused an imbalance, the strange, unsettling sense of invincibility that ironically fed into a period of deeply self-destructive behaviour. I think I was just unused to having that kind of security and it made me reckless and prone to ignoring the nagging, questioning voices within myself that might have otherwise kept me in check and guided me towards safer shores.

There's always a kind of blind zeal that is needed when you first approach making an album and despite the increasingly splintered nature of my home life and my vaunted, unrealistic ambitions I threw myself into writing what I was seeing as being a brave musical departure for Suede. The first song I wrote possibly ended up being the best thing on the record and set a hugely inflated precedent for the writing to come. It was a gentle acoustic guitar-based piece that meandered and trilled around D minor and A minor, a bitter tale of betrayal and of the revealing of truth which was possibly how, in my more desolate moments, I was beginning to view my odder, less defined new relationship with Justine. One of the premises I had for the album was for the music to speak more and so I inserted some instrumental passages and played a simple keyboard string motif over them with an eastern flavour which in the spirit of delivering a less flowery poetic record also suggested its name – 'Indian Strings'. I remember Neil and Richard coming over one day and politely ignoring the carpet of debris on the floor and sitting amongst the ash and the litter and listening to the primitive demo I had made and it providing a truly inspiring entry point for us all, and so the momentum continued for a while.

I was out in the summer house one bleary, black afternoon banging around on the keys of an old Hammond organ that I had had dragged through the garden, enjoying its reedy churchy sounds and how with an interesting, off-kilter lyric they could take on a kind of subversive edge. I started playing a descending riff that dropped in semitones from C to A and began wailing 'I can't get enough' over the top of it. As I fumbled around I found some verse chords I liked and threw the whole thing together and wrote a song that was supposed to have a kind of 'Lust For Life' sentiment, a joyous, greedy rush, unashamedly bullish and grabbing and brash. I think with the benefit of hindsight I would interpret it more as a comment on substance abuse but nevertheless it contained a kind of truth and when Neil heard it he cleverly suggested we turn it into a primal guitar piece and went about demoing it so it had more of a sort of Stooges feel that was in keeping with the original idea rather than the weird vocal and Hammond demo that I had first made. Another time Neil dropped off a cassette through my letterbox. Probably by this point my increasingly unpleasant, marginal life and personal slide into addiction was making spending time with me or in my house understandably uncomfortable to anyone not part of my muttering, dead-eyed clique – a small gaggle of gruff dealers and frazzled users and random drifters who congregated at my flat for one ugly reason. The rest of the band have always had more sense than me in that respect and Neil probably decided it was just easier to deliver it that way. The cassette had the words 'Gloopy Strings' scrawled across the top and it was a strange, gluey-sounding, pitch-bending string loop rotating around just two chords. I loved the brave simplicity and the disingenuous melodiousness of the piece and went about writing a rising vocal part which built to a falsetto chorus with something meaningless like 'she is special' sung over it. Later I changed it to something equally meaningless and it became 'She's In Fashion' and the urbane, glossy ode to vacuity was born. Once we had recorded the track it took on a poppy sheen which turned it from an odd, arty Krautrock sort of thing into a mainstream radio hit and it would eventually penetrate to an audience way beyond our fan base. It has always amused me that what became known as our lightest, most carefree musical moment was born from the ravages of utter despair and wanton abandon, a squalid, desolate baptism of degeneracy and depravity set against a back-drop of blackened cutlery and crumpled beds of burnt kitchen foil. The musical landscapes of this and other things we were exploring were suiting Neil's musicianship of course but as we wandered deeper into the writing process and the path we were taking became increasingly keyboard-led, naturally Richard started to feel somewhat marginalised and confused as to his role as the guitar player in what seemed to be becoming our electronic album. I think it was a hard time for him as apart from anything he was still very young and struggled to place himself within the shifting tectonic plates of our new world order. Added to this of course was my continued slide away from all of the band personally as our lives became polarised and our relationships began to drift and unravel. I simply didn't spend as much time hanging out with them any more and it must have been especially tough for Richard trying to express his frustrations at what must have seemed to him like a worryingly precarious situation, but nevertheless he still continued to deliver some great ideas. Brilliantly ignoring my suffocating, artificial premise for the album he turned up one day with a piece called 'Repugnant', based around a spidery arpeggio guitar part, flowing and natural and organic and everything that we said we didn't want to do but too good to ignore. As with 'Beautiful Ones' and 'Saturday Night' I wasn't happy with the chorus and so we went about writing a new one that felt more strident and direct and eventually it became a kind of karmic, agnostic hymn, where if 'God' existed it was just as part of the coiled rhythms of the everyday: prosaic, uncelestial and ordinary but nevertheless special. I called it 'Everything Will Flow' and it remains one of my favourite ever Suede songs. There were darker, more mechanical pieces too. Justine had been playing me snippets of her new album including a song I loved called 'Human'. In my deeply unmusical way I was sitting at the keyboard one day trying to rip it off but forgetting how the bass riff went and coming up with something that hinted at its dark, menacing feel but getting the notes completely wrong. I called it 'Hi Fi' and the threatening, prowling riff would later come alive when we took it into the studio, morphing into a crackling, modern pulse.

Completing a kind of trinity of misfortune by coinciding with my substance abuse and Richard's marginalisation was Neil's illness. The back-breaking world tour we had embarked on to promote the continuingly successful *Coming Up* had definitely left its scars. There's something utterly exhausting about touring: the endless repetition, the never-ending cycle of Dionysian excess and daily catharsis and the numbing stretched hours shuffling around airports and sitting on tour buses in a strange kind of heightened state waiting for something to happen. Charlie Watts' famous quote summing up his career as being 'five years' work and twenty years' hanging around' is brilliantly pithy but belies the truth that the dead time is equally if not more exhausting than the time you spend performing as you are harried like livestock from bleak blank space to bleak blank space with a permanent feeling of 'hurry up and wait' hanging over you. At some point against this back-drop of an endless, grinding tour Neil caught glandular fever and was eventually diagnosed with Chronic Fatigue Syndrome. It's a strange condition, often an umbrella term that covers a myriad of symptoms, but it leaves the person affected just too tired to perform the simplest of tasks. I don't know the full extent of what happened really, but from my perspective Neil became increasingly fragile and housebound, a development which only further atomised the ever-splintering nature of the band's interpersonal relationships and allowed me to slide further away from them in my search for oblivion, cravenly hiding my fears and frustrations under a flimsy shroud of excess.

IT DIES IN THE WHITE HOURS
OF YOUNG-LEAFED JUNE

The cones of the giant black wall-mounted speakers fluttered and the room shuddered to the overdriven stabs of the out-of-tune Fernandes guitar making the water that sat in discarded plastic beakers around the studio ripple and churn. As the distorted music thumped, tinny and broken-sounding but massively amplified by the volume level a heavily delayed vocal broke through the noise: 'Give me head / Give me head / Give me head music instead'. I nodded along, my face a mask of concentration, my eyes cast to the floor, oddly oblivious to the ridiculous lyric and occasionally glancing at the back of the producer's neck as he sat facing the other way, trying to gauge his reaction to the demo that I was presenting to him. As the last notes died there was a sticky pause as he swivelled his seat towards me, took a drag of his ever-present cigarette and finally met my gaze with his pale, tired-looking eyes. 'I don't like it,' he stated baldly, 'I'm not working on that.'

We had decided to change producers. In a spirit of bullishness and success-fuelled hubris we had blithely deemed that in order to make a different record we needed a different hand steering the ship. Our switch away from Ed wasn't completely disloyal however as by then he had moved abroad with his family which meant that working together, although of course not impossible, might prove more onerous. Regardless of such logistics his move to the States seemed to be another thing that was telling us to try someone new. Looking back I think that in many ways it was a mistake. Had we worked again with Ed our shared history and his people skills might have provided the glue to hold us all together and dragged us back into some sort of semblance of unity but maybe by that point it was just all too late. Instead we appointed a producer called Steve Osborne, a quiet, intense and softly spoken man with a broad Estuary accent and a severe 'studio tan', whom Saul had suggested as being someone who might bring a more modern edge to our sound, someone who might be able to steer us away from the more florid aspects of our back catalogue that we were keen not to revisit. We liked that he had worked on *Pills and Thrills and Bellyaches*, which had at the time seemed exciting and genre-defining and had been part of the soundtrack of my and Mat's youth, so we met him in Mayfair Studios in Primrose Hill to try out working together on a couple of tracks. I had written this strange little nursery rhyme of a song about some shadowy, fictional *femme fatale* figure called 'Savoir Faire'. It was spindly and inept and odd but Steve saw something that he thought he could develop and went about creating this brilliantly strange, off-kilter, electronic rhythm track blending live drums and samples to create a pulsing collage of sounds. It was one of those shifts that suddenly brought the song to life, turning it from a charming, inoffensive curio into a dark, grinding, predatory beast. It was exactly where I thought the album should be heading and in our excitement we decided to carry on working together. Unfortunately the energy that we had mustered for that little session didn't seem to bleed into subsequent ones. We reconvened at Eastcote Studios just off the top of Ladbroke Grove and in that dark, leaden summer of 1998 proceeded to fall apart. Whenever I think about Steve Osborne I'm always charged with the niggling desire to pick up the phone and apologise to him. I think he saw the band at its absolute nadir – dislocated, uninspired and unwell – and he probably views me as someone very different from the person who I like to flatter myself I really am. By this point my addictions had drifted on to desperate levels and my motivations for making music were completely secondary revealing a weak and selfish side to my nature which I'm sure Steve saw on too many occasions. As our relationship was still new he had none of the back story or the shared history and was confronted with a barely functioning band but appointed to try to inspire them to make an album – a Herculean task at the best of times. My addictions, Richard's musical marginalisation and Neil's absence through illness created a kind of bizarre climate of dysfunction which meant that I think for vast swathes of the sessions Mat was the only band member present in the studio as we left Steve stranded and with little input and forced to try to be creative on his own. In a way this unusual dynamic accounts for the unique feel of *Head Music* which maybe has an odd kind of merit but I often wonder what that album would have been like if we had been a properly functioning band. I always think of it as half a great record – some of the songs like 'He's Gone' and 'Indian Strings' and 'Everything Will Flow' are amongst our best – but unfortunately by this point our collective judgement was severely impaired and so we allowed it to be weakened by a motley, ragged little family of runts like 'Crack In The Union Jack', 'Asbestos' and the risible title track. The obsessive levels of quality control that we had applied over previous albums had disappeared, partly as an element of a new manifesto but mainly through a creeping tide of laziness – a slack 'it'll turn out okay in the end' sort of attitude that drilled a fatal flaw of disrespect into the foundations of our work. Ed's absence meant that there was no one present who really knew how, or indeed wanted, to make a classic Suede record, and to be fair that was the point of hiring Steve but it meant that the album took on a kind of untethered, patchy character, brilliant in places but weak and embarrassing in others as we fumbled around for a new identity. Inevitably we made the usual serial mistakes in what we chose for B-sides, consigning one of the most sensitive, beautiful moments of that era, a song called 'Leaving', to those lonely, tumble-weed terrains. It was supposed to be a kind of message of strength from a friend for Justine who at the time was quite lonely and sad, stalled in the dying embers of a fading relationship but lacking the clarity and courage to move beyond it. I suppose it was intended to have a kind of *carpe diem* feel, and to contain a thread of hope and a call for change. I'm not sure if I ever even bothered playing her the song, and she would probably hate its vaguely sentimental, cloying feel if she heard it, but sometimes you can write things about people and never intend that they actually listen to it, their role sometimes just being a vehicle to generate an idea. One particularly contentious track that did end up making the cut was something Neil had written on his own called 'Elephant Man'. When he first played me the demo I thought it was quite a brilliant piece of honest self-deprecating songwriting. I interpreted it as his comment on his illness and thought therefore that it had an integrity and a power and bullishly insisted that it was included on the album, much to Saul's chagrin, enjoying the novelty that for the first time on a Suede album some of its lyrics would not be written by me. Looking back I think in my twisted, idealism I may have ignored the song's slightly oversimplistic, chanting, playground-taunt sort of character which now seems to give it a disposable edge but in those gloomy, sunless afternoons of 1998 it spoke to me as a snap-shot of our lives and therefore contained its own kind of truth.

Back towards the tail-end of the *Coming Up* campaign we had written 'He's Gone'. It was a beautiful, graceful thing which borrowed the feel of one of those old torch-song standards like 'My Way' and charted the slow disintegration of my and Sam's relationship. We had bumbled around under the plane trees and on the scruffier pavements of west London for many years, her candid wit and her unaffected honesty acting as a counterbalance to my frothy quixotry and providing a dynamic that held us together and provided the emotional back-drop to some wonderful times. Locked together though we had slid into a mutual pit of addiction which of course in many ways created a further level of unhealthy co-dependency and we found ourselves drifting within a strange limbo, our emotions deadened through substance abuse but our ability to instigate change impeded. Even though I wasn't able to express it at the time I think that I began to feel guilty for dragging her into this hell with me. I felt I had been terribly glib and irresponsible as I convinced myself that it was all still some twisted extension of my work, that I was still somehow playing at what I was doing, but for her the consequences seemed much less superficial and far more real as she became increasingly damaged by the testing, harrowing journey. In 'He's Gone' I used the same device as for 'My Insatiable One' years earlier where I switched perspectives and talked about myself in the third person to weave together a grief-laden tale of loss and sadness that still moves me. Over a decade later I would sing it at the Albert Hall during our come-back show as a dedication to my friend Jesse who tragically had just killed himself, the words and the tone seeming somehow equally as relevant and the fact that Jesse was my and Sam's beautiful, much missed mutual friend seeming to justify the act. Back when recording the song, Steve Osborne had taken its fairly trad nature and modernised it with delays and keyboards and made it one of the outstanding moments on the album and one of the handful of tracks of which I am still very proud.

As we scrabbled around trying to finish the album it was again put to us by Saul that we were still missing the first single. 'She's In Fashion' although bristling with cross-over chart pizzazz seemed too breezy and light to be the opening statement from a band known for releasing singles with grit and drama and so, keen not to confuse the fan-base, Richard and Neil and myself busied ourselves with the often dutiful process that is 'writing a single', something that if done wrong can feel forced and formulaic, a dull litany of check-lists and empty musical gestures ... which is how we came up with the anthem to meaninglessness that was 'Electricity', an uninspired box-ticker with a 'big' chorus and a 'gutsy' verse, a waste of four minutes and thirty-nine seconds of everyone's time that could almost have been created by one of the novel-writing machines that Julia operated in *1984*. This shouty, pointless, hollow song signifying absolutely nothing when released of course, like its equally vacuous cousin 'Stay Together', crashed into the top five and enjoyed saturation levels of mainstream exposure while genuine gems like 'The Wild Ones' and 'Everything Will Flow' floundered and flopped on the margins. Ah well, such is life. I think my biggest criticism of our work during this period though would have to rest on my lyric writing. My unforgivable lack of focus and drift into selfishness had blunted my previously sharp powers of observation and initiated a slow slide into self-parody. I think the general laziness of the lyrics to this album were responsible for a hugely resonating dissection of my style of writing where critics started to correctly see that I was regurgitating ideas to such an extent that it felt that all one needed for a Suede song was to mention a few stock phrases like 'nuclear skies' and 'hired cars' and 'pigs by motorways' or something and you could make a fairly decent fist of your own version. I justified it at the time as a shift away from focusing on the words towards the music in a vague chase for some sort of modernity but of course it was never going to be interpreted like that. It's a legacy that I still find myself wrestling with and one born from my indolent approach on that record. I think previously I had just tip-toed the right side of the line, keen to develop a specific lexicon and tone that would create a Suede landscape but as my mind became dulled by addiction and cravings I allowed it to be overused and what was previously a strong lyrical identity became a tired, clichéd reliance on reusable ideas lending the whole album a patina of uninspired vacuity, which had huge, unexpected consequences going forward into the next album and is something which I deeply, deeply regret.

There were some pertinent moments of truth of course, like the searingly bleak documenting of the sad state of my life called 'Down'. It was something that I had written myself on a baby grand piano that I had bought from one of the antique shops on Golborne Road. I had put it in the dusty, disused spare room that looked out on to the old red-brick wall which hid the clattering train lines. Beyond that the Westway rumbled and soughed and the tower blocks of the Harrow Road estates loomed against the back-lit skies with a monolithic, science-fiction grace. It was a conventional ballad which Neil later suggested we lend the feel of 'Mother' by John Lennon but when I plonked out the first few chords one cheerless twilit afternoon it had more of a leaden, ploddy sound which echoed the tragedy of the lyric. It was a grim self-portrait, a dark vision of myself as a spent, weakened man. 'Hey you chase the day away / Hey you draw the blinds and blow your mind away' went the chorus: a sad, honest snap-shot of the desperate truth of my life. This painfully candid self-reflection came in the aftermath of a truly horrific episode which acted eventually as a pivotal watershed in my life. The evening in question was the tail-end of a smear of days in which Alan, Sam and myself had taken our levels of consumption to new uncharted territories. Trembling and shaking and gurning we had pushed ourselves way beyond what was usually acceptable, even for us. At one point Sam staggered upstairs to use the bathroom when suddenly Alan and I heard a heavy thump echoing through the ceiling followed by a series of strange knocking sounds. Sensing something was terribly wrong we sprinted upstairs to find Sam convulsing on the floorboards in the throes of a horrific fit, her mouth frothing with white foam and spittle and her eyes rolling back and fluttering in furious, terrifying spasms. As horror and blind white-knuckled panic gripped me I somehow found an instinct deep within myself and proceeded to pump her heart with the heel of my palms and breathe heavily into her mouth with mine until with a gasping, shuddering breath she came back to us. For one unbelievably harrowing moment all of our lives were hanging suspended by a gossamer thread and we had glimpsed something that was so dark as to really defy description. I will never forget it and the consequences of what might have happened that night still torment me to this day and sometimes still spool within my mind's eye in a horrific, circling loop.

WE DON'T HAVE TO
LIVE LIKE THIS

Dragging the agenda back to the dreary machinery of the music business seems so trivial and petty after reliving that awful, awful moment but despite the horrors and the looming spectre of tragedy, despite the ragged, faltering journey, despite the flaws in the record and the disjointed, joyless way in which it was made, despite the huge unanswered questions dangling threateningly over the band we had somehow, somehow managed to complete it and deliver something which everyone pretended they were happy with. When faced with promoting an album there is a point at which the whole team – band, record company, management, publishers, press people and promoters – are all forced to get behind it. The period of reflection and questioning ends and it becomes part of everyone's jobs to convince themselves and everyone around them that they love the product they are expected to work with and to spread enthusiasm in order to try to inspire industry confidence, hence the proliferation of meaningless, platitudinous phrases like 'it's the best thing they've ever done' or 'it's a massive return to form' being uttered every time certain bands put out a new record. It's part of the dull, uninspiring mechanics of releasing records as, with some notable exceptions, they are often released by dull, uninspired people who are unable to express themselves in language beyond cliché, and indeed in some ways the industry requires this lack of imagination. Despite the seismic changes imposed on it by the digital revolution it's still a heavy, lumbering beast that finds it hard to take on new ideas but that steady inevitability is how it ambles ever forward. I had decided to call the album *Head Music*, enjoying its oblique, modern tone which suggested to me the cleaner lines of the sort of music we were trying to make. I think to be honest it may have been a phrase that I had heard Justine use once when describing something and magpie-like I had grabbed it and scribbled it down in the cramped forest of phrases in my notebook.

There is also always a bit of a delay in how the industry and the press and the public receive records which means that you are often either trying to atone for the mistakes of the previous one or bathing in its success. As *Head Music* had followed what was commercially our most successful record yet there was a definite tide of ebullience that greeted its release and we were offered headline festival slots and saturation press coverage and record shop prioritisation like never before as we embarked on the nascent steps of the campaign. We had reached the stage where the fizz and clamour around the release had given us the reach to be able to conduct a series of press conferences rather than scraps of bitty interviews to separate papers and so we sat there on a podium on a few occasions like prize turnips hiding behind our sunglasses and laughing at the surreal perversity of the whole thing as the shutters clicked and a small thicket of jostling microphones awaited our utterances. Emerging from the stifling maze of self-doubt and struggle that is inherent in making any album is always actually quite an exciting time; there's a period of a month or so between delivering the record and it meeting the cold, hard edges of the real world when you always genuinely think you have made something special, something that might just potentially connect in a way that you have never connected before and you are filled with a temporary short-lived effervescence, a willing self-deception partly built around hope but also because promoting it is impossible unless you genuinely believe in it – you have to ignore its flaws in order that you can get on with your job. And so I allowed myself to be sucked into that shallow fantasy, believing the promises of dizzying projected sales figures and untold success that the industry was murmuring in my ear like a coquettish lover whispering sweet nothings, but it was all just a brittle illusion, a house of cards that began to tumble and fall around us once everything had inevitably flattened and lost its fizz. The small string of anarchic fan-club shows that had kicked off the campaign would have been exciting even if we hadn't turned up as the level of anticipation was so feverish by that point that my shortcomings as a performer due to physical weakness and addiction were not fully exposed. In truth I was only half there and operated on auto-pilot, never fully able to give myself to the bacchanalian parade of borrowed insanity that you need to surrender yourself to in order to put on a great show. As Turner says in Nic Roeg's famous film: 'The only performance that makes it, that makes it all the way is the one that achieves madness'. When we started to tour properly however we encountered real problems. After a while it became clear that Neil was simply too unwell to continue with us on the road. Despite our hopes to the contrary, his crippling illness still meant that he was spending vast swathes of time bed-bound and his doctors had advised that the sapping, wearying process of touring was the last thing that their patient needed. It must have been a terrible time for him but it was a hard time for me too as despite feeling guilty about it and understanding the reasons I couldn't help feeling let down and not knowing how to express my frustrations they would often bubble over as anger. Unable to return to being a four-piece as so much of the set now required keyboards we drafted in Alex Lee whom we had met when Strangelove toured with us back in 1995. They had been a fantastic support band, one of those whose dramatic, emotional songs come alive on stage. Their singer Patrick Duff was a brilliant performer – confrontational and utterly engaging – and between sound checks and during tour dead-time he had revealed himself as a surprisingly warm and lovely man and one with whom I am glad to say I am still friends today. Alex was always the musical rock to Patrick's erratic intensity; a fine guitar player and super-talented all-round musician he flew out to the show at very short notice and with a scant amount of rehearsal proceeded to deal with the overwhelming task with an air of bewildering calm, steadying our ship as we bobbed about on those choppy, churning seas. And so we limped on but this time I had a sickening feeling that our wounds might be mortal. Neil joining the band had given us a balance and a chemistry and his musical influence was a key element in the kind of record that *Head Music* had become; in many ways I felt as though we had almost built it around him and suddenly to find an empty space where he once was seemed to somehow mock the album's integrity and undermine the whole campaign with a fatal fault-line. It was to become another bullet in the gun that would eventually kill us.

PART FIVE

I DROWN IN THE DRUMMING PLOUGHLAND

As I gazed out over the quiet lawn and beyond the thicket of birch trees that screened the house from the road I sipped at my tea and rewound the cassette tape. The traffic soughed gently along the High Road outside that backed on to the hedged borders of the garden with the occasional whoosh and rumble which scattered the blossom of late spring and softly punctuated the rhythm of the day; a strange reminder of the existence of other human life, no matter how dislocated, no matter how removed. I had rented what I suppose would be called a 'granny flat', a small annexed self-contained house that I was using as a temporary writing retreat in a place called Chipstead, a sleepy little Surrey village full of gruff golf-playing traders and their bored pony-riding wives nestled in the heart of the stockbroker belt. It was a move designed to supply as much isolation and as much distance as possible from the temptations and frenetic pulse of the city, providing me with space and calm and somewhere I could gather my thoughts and begin work on what would become our last album together. Well, at least until the next life. Still not having passed my test, once my driver John had dropped me off I was stranded within the countryside's leafy clutches, willingly exiled to a strange lonely Arcadian world of drifting bucolic solitude and solemn pastoral reflection. Between long bouts hammering away at my manual typewriter and squawking into my microphone I would clear my cluttered, deafened head by putting on my scruffy old Vans trainers and tramping along the bramble-lined pathways, losing myself in long afternoons of quiet meditation that only a spot of bracing wandering can provide. I was trying to escape from the gloomy litter-strewn rooms and the paranoia and the shimmer of threat that had become life in the city and especially from the abject horrors that had defined the genesis of *Head Music*, realising a little too late that what I was throwing away as I glibly shook out the contents of the binbags was actually my life. What I found however as I traipsed along the muddy paths and under the knotted branches of the horse-chestnut trees was a different kind of truth from the one I was expecting. The countryside, I was slowly rediscovering, rather than being some idealised idyll, some pleasant, inoffensive John

Constable painting brought to life, was actually rife with the same kind of tawdry secrets as the city and I would often happen upon torn, muddied pages of porn magazines stashed secretly under bushes or the telltale litter of used drug paraphernalia, stark reminders that people will seek out the stink of life no matter where they are. Sometimes while ambling through a Disney-esque wooded glade I would be confronted with sour graveyards of rusted white enamel fridges and sodden ripped furniture and broken children's car seats: shameful, discarded, fly-tipped hoards sat stark and surreal against the quiet, sober beauty of nature. Slowly I began to sketch out a very rough idea for an album set in a strange rural hinterland circumscribed by B roads, a world of roadkill and overgrown concrete paths and rotting animals – a kind of dark, Ted Hughes-tinged vision that portrayed the countryside as a real place rather than some romanticised Claude Lorrain water-colour. I had become slightly obsessed with Ballard's brilliantly dystopian *Concrete Island*, an updated version of *Robinson Crusoe* in which a man finds himself marooned within an enclosure, hemmed in by motor-ways and crash barriers and forced to live in an unseen, liminal world of waist-high grass and rusted, broken car parts. The imagery of the story began to resonate powerfully with me as I tramped around the green belt and always stayed in my mind. Even though the clarity of the idea might eventually become diluted it would be revisited nearly twenty years later with *The Blue Hour*. I wonder what it is about authors like Ballard and Orwell that inspires so many musicians. For me there is something both profound and stylish about their writing and about the worlds that they create, an alluring blend of depth and surface. Both ruthlessly dissect the carcass of the human condition but do so within a charged and highly stylised arena. *1984*, for all its contemporary relevance, is a simple love story spotlit against a mannered back-drop and Ballard's neo-Futurist imagery always seems to me to be so rich with theatre that you can almost see the stage sets. I suppose it's this palpable drama that musicians respond to, channelling it into those simplistic brushstrokes that make up most rock songs.

Rather like Orwell when he was researching *Down and Out in Paris and London*, after a couple of weeks of isolation and ever-darkening thought in my rural bolt-hole I would eventually run out of food and having had enough called John and got him to pick me up and take me back to London. John was a wonderful discovery. I'd met him through Saul as he had worked for him for a while when Nude was bustling with too many employees. When I'd decided I needed a driver and couldn't face more untold hours making small talk with random cabbies I'd bought a car and met John and we had got on like the proverbial blazing house. He is the perfect person with whom to spend long journeys; he is kind and respectful and very funny, possessing a bone-dry, self-deprecating Tottenham fan's wit and the flattened, drawling vowels of a broad Estuary accent. He's the sort of person about whom no one has a bad word despite the fact that in public on more than one occasion he's been mistaken for Ronnie Wood. He has such an air of peaceful serenity that if it were suddenly announced on the news that Jesus had returned to earth in the form of a Spurs fan from Luton I wouldn't be in the least surprised. We became great friends during those strange, in-between years of the early noughties and I'm happy to say that we still are today. He would pick me up at the cottage and I would throw my bags in the back and we would wind our way up through the tarmacked streets and the ring roads of south London chattering easily about music or football while half listening as The Sophtware Slump or Deserter's Songs played on the car stereo. Eventually the car would putter into the familiar magnolia-lined street and he would drop me back at my new home, a white stucco-fronted townhouse in Northumberland Place, two streets parallel to Moorhouse Road where I had lived through the gaudy dramas that had inspired the songs on the debut album a decade earlier. It was a classic, elegant London townhouse with a mansard roof and beautiful wrought-iron Juliet balconies, all high-corniced ceilings and period details: an estate agent's dream. Fortunately I had managed to buy it before the whole area turned into Knightsbridge and became ruined by the hedge-funders building double basements and cynically viewing the houses as 'investment opportunities' rather than homes, when there was still a wonderful, welcoming community bustling with artists and actors and charming old-school diplomats and the strange, fun conversations you had were about film and theatre rather than dry discussions about 'pounds per square foot' and 'maximising dead space'. I saw buying the house as very symbolic of my attempt to escape from the horrors of substance dependency and despite there being a short period of bleed-over tried to use the change in address as a way to shift into a cleaner phase in our lives. The house was bright and welcoming and beautiful, somehow the sort of place where kids have happy childhoods, and I so wanted to not let the whole atmosphere slide into the slurry of dirt and addiction and ugliness that had characterised Westbourne Park Villas. There were also spare rooms and we heard that a good friend of ours, my sometime make-up artist Tania Rodney, needed to move out of her flat so we offered her one. Tania is a bright and shrewd girl from Yorkshire, bluff and blunt at times but sharp and funny with it and always lovely and perhaps, most important of all, not in any way a part of the smeary, dissolute demi-monde of London users which I was so desperate to escape. Over the years she became a dear friend and through those early years when we all lived in Northumberland Place, in a very passive, subtle way, kept us all in check and less likely to veer off the path and back into some ruinously messy state. I suppose it's not very interesting to read about how someone might strive towards a state of abstinence; it doesn't fit with the mythical Jungian archetype of the wayward artist – the bullshit, theme-park 'guitar hero' rock and roll lie. The irony is that I've just spent a whole part of this book charting my own spiralling decline into a parody of an addicted rock star but I have always hated those trite clichés that so many people secretly love, hoping that true artistry has less to do with JD and Harleys and more to do with having the bravery to document a truth in your life. If that truth happens to involve burnt foil and psychosis then so be it but if it happens to be something smaller and less salacious then there is equally valuable material therein. I believe that there are always fascinating songs hiding even in the least likely places; sometimes they are just lurking in small domestic frictions and misunderstandings and it's only a lazy writer who can't be bothered to look for them there.

Inevitably I have profound regrets about my dalliances with addiction and substance abuse. Although at the time I justified my wayward recklessness as an almost essential part of a career making interesting music now I can't help but think that that approach is just an excuse; a feeble apology for my weak, bestial gluttony. When I think of all the wasted, drifting days and the bleary, numb morning-afters it frightens me slightly and I ponder how I could have put all that dead time to use. And what had I really been doing? Just pursuing some tired, romanticised vision of the decadent, rakish libertine. There is often a confusion in people's minds that links hedonism with creativity and at some level I was probably stupidly guilty of this. The assumption that addiction and intemperance are somehow essentially creative states seems to arise from the fact that historically so many creative people have led dissolute lifestyles. In fact I would propose that the link is more likely due to creative people having the kind of inquisitive minds that lead them to explore the landscape of altered states but once they have arrived there their creativity is rarely heightened or enhanced. Of course there are anomalies which seem to disprove this as there always are but looking back at my career and using my own experiences as a sounding board I have a sinking feeling that had I abstained it simply would have improved my work. I can often hear the weakness and the lack of focus in our early records and am sometimes tortured by a need to revisit them and correct the 'mistakes'. But as Heraclitus' famous aphorism reminds us, 'No man steps in the same river twice for it is not the same river and he is not the same man', and I realise that going back would be ultimately futile, an exercise in addressing some vanity that would mean little to anyone else. Once these moments have passed they have passed. Also I remind myself that, as with people, it's often the flaws and blemishes which make music more real and imbue it with a beauty. 'To err is human' as someone much cleverer than me once said, and surely an exploration of the state of humanity, beautiful despite and sometimes because of its flaws, is what art ultimately strives to achieve.

My work out in the wilds of Surrey was feeding back into writing with Richard and Neil in London and as often happens in those first flushes of a new session we hit on some early gems. I'd converted the top floor of the house in Northumberland Place into a writing room and had my baby grand hoisted in one day much to the consternation of the agog neighbours who anxiously gathered out on the pavement to crane their necks and watch, probably slightly horrified that a musician was moving into the street and possibly some of them being aware of my reputation as one of the less savoury ones. It was a beautiful room with a tiled west-facing balcony that provided a panorama of church spires and sixties tower blocks stretching out over west London and when I was at a creative dead end I would just sit out there on an old creosoted garden bench and smoke and gaze at the majesty of the city laid out before me. One day I was flopped there mulling over my and Sam's drifting, fraying lives and I started finding words for a song that used the endlessness of the sea to describe the distance between two people and I named it 'Oceans'. It was a simple track with a slightly skittering, rising verse and a lifting chorus but it spoke a truth to me. It was about the slow, incremental death of a relationship, one which doesn't crash and burn with a glamorous, tragic fire but one which ends noiselessly in lonely, tiny pieces. I was trying to express something of the quiet ruin of long-term estrangement – difficult to do when music itself needs the motor of drama and fire to work, but I like that it contains this meaning and it still moves me today. It was an understated but important piece of writing for me that made me again very conscious of there being just as much, if not more, power and beauty in the quiet little moments of life's theatre as in the big showy ones and that's a tenet that still informs much of my writing today.

One of the tracks I was working on down in Surrey was something Richard had given me with the working title of 'Plucky', a spidery, intricate guitar piece that I immediately loved. I wrote around it a song about my friend Alan, teasing out the detail of his charming gaucherie and celebrating it as an essential part of his wonderful, unique character. I called it 'Cheap'. Alan has been an evergreen presence in my life as anyone who has been kind enough to invest time in these two books will realise, dipping in and out, flicking his ash, colouring everything with his bizarre clash of old-school charm and ruthless, maniacal hedonism. He's one of those people who never fails to fascinate me, the complex, intertwined tendrils of his life always threatening to spill over and never failing to deliver an almost script-written theatre which is often nail-biting and hilarious in equal measures. I assume like all relationships that work on some level we offer each other elements that we don't ourselves possess. As a writer and an artist I can only wonder at his genuine charisma and odd, off-kilter magnetism – qualities which I have tried to emulate through my work but secretly I suspect that personally I don't actually possess. In many ways he has been the most constant in my series of muses and as such has a unique position in the pantheon of my work – a friend who has seen the best and the worst of me and all the points in between and who to this day never fails to inspire.

The brink of disaster that we had teetered over while making *Head Music* was clearly something we were keen to not return to and so we were determined for this new album to be more of an organic rock record, light and pastoral in places but eschewing the murky, synthetic urban dead ends that we had blindly marched down while making the previous one. As always there was the feeling that when making Suede records we were swinging between polarities: that we would start to make the new one with the premise that it should in some way oppose the last. The swing away from *Head Music* to this new album was something that I wanted to make the most dramatic of all as I began to build up an idea that the new record should be everything that *Head Music* wasn't: quiet, gentle, intricate and sensitive. I think by this point in our career the persona of Suede was in many ways beyond our control; the image of the band that had been projected back to us over the last decade had inevitably become distorted and still seemed very different from the one that we believed to be true. It began to feel suffocating and uncomfortable, imprisoned as we were within the narrow definition of how many people saw us, which was as this fey, furtive, urban, slightly vacuous band. Of course these were stereotypes that we had been at various points guilty of propagating but like many bands we found ourselves limited and frustrated by the confining expectations of our label. There was a feeling in the camp that we wanted to subvert the perceptions of who we were and go about making an album that the fans wouldn't expect and which many of them might not like. Unfortunately we succeeded rather too well. They were all fine starting points that initiated the record and if they had been followed through with urgency and stamina and determination might have produced something wonderful but unfortunately events would conspire against us and what were good intentions would slide into the muddy puddle of lackadaisical confusion.

Neil had been contributing some pieces but he was obviously still very frail, valiantly trying to resist the ongoing ruin of his condition but slowly becoming less and less able to work. I think we had all hoped that given time away from the ravages of touring he would have had the space and peace to recuperate and that now we had moved into the more genteel climes of the writing phase he would softly improve and wander back into the fold and everything would be lovely again. One day though I was sitting listening to 'Feeling Yourself Disintegrate' and the phone rang. It was Charlie asking if he and Neil could come over. I could tell from his deadened, flattened tone that it was something serious. My stomach lurched with a sickening feeling and ten minutes later there was a bang at the door. Charlie and Neil shuffled furtively into the lounge and Neil stood there, his eyes cast down on the floor, as he quietly told me that he was leaving the band. I knew that by this point it wasn't something that was up for discussion, that it was a tortuous decision that he would have arrived at after months of deliberation and internal debate, that by now there was nothing that could change his mind, that he saw this as the only way in which he could grasp back some semblance of health. I remember the meeting being brief as I nodded and blankly accepted his decision, my mask of cold indifference hiding the conflicting, broiling feelings of fear and sadness and dread that were surging inside me. When these pivotal moments in my career have happened I have often reacted to them in a seemingly very unemotional way, burying my hurt and my panic behind a carapace of professionalism probably as some sort of self-defence mechanism that allows me to avoid tides of overwhelming feeling, but with both Bernard's and Neil's departure what I felt beyond the gnawing feeling of abandonment was the sad loss of a friend. What Neil probably saw as I let him out of my house and gruffly said goodbye was a downcast, vaguely embittered man trying to bluff his way through the situation with a veneer of practicality. In reality my world was reeling and I knew that at some level the band had been dealt a blow from which it might never recover.

FIVE GET INTO A FIX

The starlings soared high above the Wealdland clay, criss-crossing over the cars that puttered along the A2100, wheeling against the currents of the high wind that blew eastwards across the South Downs. Far below in a darkened, fetid, baffled drum booth in the live room of a studio the atmosphere was close. The perfumed smoke from the Nag Champa incense stick coiled in the air and mingled the scent of sandalwood with the heavy fug of cigarette fumes as the rack-tom thumped and the cymbals splashed. His brow knitted, Simon sat at his kit and resentfully played along to the drum machine's skittish, loping, hip-hop groove, his face a mask of passive aggression, his discomfort palpable. 'That sounds phat, man,' said the producer in his light Tennessee drawl, finally ending the ordeal by turning off the beat-box and wandering back to the control room leaving us alone staring sullenly at the floor, our ears ringing in the sudden, cloying silence. 'Well, what do you think?' I asked hopefully. Simon took a drag of his B&H and as he raised his head our eyes finally locked. 'Brett, this sounds like shit and we shouldn't be working with him.'

As the tyres of the gun-metal grey Mercedes SEC crunched against the gravel John and I pulled into the car park and took in the sight of a row of single-storey, red-brick dwellings which arched round and formed a courtyard with the main building, a large pitch-roofed wood and brick structure with gabled windows. This was Parkgate Studios, a residential complex in Battle down in Sussex not a million miles from the dreary suburban scrub-lands where Mat and I grew up and somewhere we had chosen as a place to record the new album. The ever-shifting cast now included Alex Lee as a full-time member of the band, replacing Neil and temporarily adding a thrust to our spluttering momentum with his talent and artistry. We had appointed someone fairly unknown to produce the album – a slight-looking red-headed American called Tony Hoffer who bore more than a passing resemblance to a young Woody Allen. Saul especially was always very keen that we were seen to be rein-venting ourselves, knowing that fickle public attention will wander unless it is permanently presented with something that it believes is shiny and new, and with the fervour of an A&R man exploring the thresholds of one of the only ways in which they are allowed to be creative had presented us with a flurry of unusual names in an attempt to steer the whole project away from the narrow borders of predictability. It's certainly true that by this point we were confused about the kind of record we wanted to make. We should have had the strength of vision to follow our original idea through and make an intricate, delicate acoustic album that the best moments of the demos like 'Cheap' and 'Oceans' had been hinting at. But for a band like Suede that had tasted the bubble and fizz of chart success such a record was never going to be permitted, caught up as we were in an inelegant, downward-spiralling scrabble to still be part of the mainstream, our position in which had become inevitably more precarious as the fissures and fault lines had begun to reveal themselves. To be fair there was a creeping, burning feeling within the whole camp that we desperately needed some new ideas, that the Suede clichés had become smother-ing and uninspiring and that to progress at all we needed to subvert them and destroy our own myth. Unfortunately though we had been too unsteadied by Neil's departure, the relative critical failure of *Head Music* and the legacy of my substance abuse to really be able to see through any successful reinvention as we desperately bandied around ridiculous, unwieldy phrases like 'electronic folk' to suggest an unlikely new direction. Personally my long period of addiction and dependency during the making of *Head Music* had bled into a fraught struggle for abstinence and then a period of relative sobriety but the whole experience had created a fresh kind of psychic imbalance in me, leaving me with a kind of artificial zeal and a strange delusion of strength and health which resulted in a phase where I frantically tried to prove to myself and to the world that I had moved on. The result was some very bad musical judgements and for a while a brief, ill-considered affair with an ugly blonde hairstyle which I thought at the time implied some sort of protean energy but which really, as my wife quite rightly now laughingly points out, made me look like a plasterer.

Thinking that he could inject some of the off-kilter pop sensibility present in his work with Beck and Air we had met up with Tony Hoffer and got on really well. Tony is a very smart guy, extremely talented and diligent and great fun to be with but, to put it simply, he just wasn't right for Suede. Sometimes these things just don't work out despite how much everyone wants them to. For a session that was to end so disastrously though there were plenty of light episodes along the way and the mood was surprisingly jovial. A bizarre moment came when Tony thought we should fly in a big-shot LA keyboard player to nail a part. Once an agreement was made and flights were booked the musician's management duly presented ours with a surreal contractual requirement stipulating his need for 'twenty-four-hour access to roast lamb', something that still makes me chuckle to this day. The levity of the session belied a creeping sense of panic though. Tony's musical language was very different from ours: he spoke in much more technical, less song-based terms and it always felt that we were pulling in different directions, him trying to tease out some sort of light, modern groove-based pop sensibility and us being too set in our ways to be able to respond properly resulting in an incompatible mesh of ideas. To be fair to Tony his remit from the record company was probably to try to stretch the band and drag it towards unfamiliar territories but I think Suede is one of those bands that evolves incrementally and on its own terms, and so putting on such unfamiliar clothes was always going to come across as a bit like a middle-aged man trying to dress like a teenager. Looking back it's incredibly sad that we all felt such a burning need to subvert our oeuvre. It's almost that by this point we had become a bit embarrassed by what we had done in the past, so much so that it seemed we were trying to wriggle away from it like a squirming child trying to escape the suffocating clutches of their grandmother. We wanted to distance ourselves so much that we went about what effectively amounted to a campaign of self-sabotage, coming up with mawkish, deliberately saccharine songs like 'Positivity' as attempts to confound the fan base and to somehow realign and reinvent ourselves. I recall writing the lyrics to that song in a rehearsal room in London and being filled with a strange kind of truculent, bloody-minded rush knowing that what I simplistically saw as the archetypal Suede fan would hate its sentiment, seeing its values as being diametrically opposed to the conventional mores of our canon. It almost got to a strange point where when making judgement calls we would ask ourselves, 'What would Suede do?' and then proceed to do the exact opposite regardless of whether the decision was actually the right one or not. By this time it felt like we were wandering through a wilderness of mirrors, trying to catch a glimpse towards the right path within a bewildering barrage of reflections. And round and round we went getting tighter and tighter up to the nail, submerged within that strange bunker mentality which drifting, untethered, unmonitored residential-studio time can often instill. More cumbersome hybrid songs appeared – sensitive acoustic pieces like 'Untitled' and 'When The Rain Falls' – which we ruined by trying to drag them into a territory into which they just didn't want to be dragged, adding synthesisers where they weren't needed and drum machines where none were required, frantically trying to force them to adopt some sort of modernity like a tragic dad trying to dress like his son. By the time we had struggled back up the M23 and cleared our heads and listened to the monitor mixes everyone felt that the mess of ideas pointed to the fact that we had got it all horribly wrong.

We took the dizzying, drastic step of deciding to start again from scratch, reconvening at Townhouse Studios and this time hiring Stephen Street as a safe pair of hands to try to guide us back towards the shores of sanity. Stephen had of course worked with the Smiths on most of their seminal records and so collaborating with him was in many ways an exciting experience for me, embedded as those records were within the very fabric of my childhood. His track record speaks for itself and I very much enjoyed his clarity and drive which were utterly galvanising. In many ways though it's a shame that his work with us coincided with our career nadir as I feel that the failure of the record prevented any further journey together. By this point we had possibly become tired of the songs and even Stephen's great skills couldn't quite tease out in us that wild-eyed excitement that is always required as we dutifully ran through what were in some cases the third or fourth version of the same track, a dulling, colourless process that I think bled through somehow into the final recordings. When assessing that album I'm always slightly sorry that yet again we ignored the real gems from that period – 'Simon', 'Cheap' and 'Oceans' – and instead bewilderingly decided to include insipid trudge-throughs like 'One Hit To The Body', the sort of song that wouldn't have even been considered as a B-side in the early days, our acuity muddied and our perspective utterly clouded. Looking back with the self-righteousness of hindsight it seems staggering to me that somehow a track like 'Simon' didn't make it on to the album. It was arguably the last great song we wrote during this period and even though conceived as more of an interim piece in terms of quality and ambition and sweep it was a completely different beast to most of the runts that did end up making the cut. I suppose we saw its inherent baroque grandeur as too much part of the *Dog Man Star* sort of sound-world we were trying to disown. Sadly by this point even though we thought we knew what we didn't want I don't think we had any idea of what we did want. When I look at this period I sometimes think it's more a failure of curation rather than a failure of creativity: we had allowed the manifesto to dictate the form, replacing good songs with weaker ones because they fitted the remit of the record better. Whenever we have released albums there have always been moments of quiet panic that have consumed us and those around us and distorted our judgement. At these times we have tended to lack the bravery to let the more delicate material speak, deciding instead to give the more formulaic songs a platform: the singles, the meaty-sounding rock tracks, the kind that have worked for us in the past. Unfortunately with this record the ones that fitted that description were, despite exceptions, decidedly weaker than on previous albums which meant that below-par rockers like 'Streetlife' had pushed aside wistful tracks like 'Cheap'. Also I think that my continuing, unpoliced meddling in the musical side of things had real consequences in weakening our work. The songs I wrote for *Head Music* and *A New Morning* just don't have the same blend of melody and tension that those written with Bernard and Richard and Neil have. I didn't understand the importance of what has become known as 'the Suede chord' – that moment of unexpected, jarring drama that lots of our best work contains. Instead my chord sequences tended to be anodyne and simplistic, often just polite accompaniments to the narrative and the top-line melodies.

There were a couple of moments on the album though of which I'm still proud: the barrelling, driving guitar rock of 'Obsessions', one of Richard's many great lost pieces to which I penned a kind of modernised version of Gershwin's 'They Can't Take That Away From Me' and Mat's only other great moment so far as a co-writer, the reflective 'Lost In TV', a song that extended some of *Dog Man Star*'s themes of disintegrated lives lived through television programmes and fictional characters. But it was all too little and all too late. By the time we had put the desultory finishing touches on the album we were so exhausted by its onerous, enervating gestation that we had simply lost all enthusiasm, our energy ground down by a kind of 'song fatigue' whereby we had become so familiar with the music that it had lost all meaning, rather like the phenomenon of repeating the same word over and over and finding that you can no longer really hear it in the same way as before. With the clarity of hindsight *A New Morning* should never have been released. To be fair to Saul he did have serious misgivings but by this point his influence had waned as Nude had folded in a kind of post-nineties hangover and we had been acquired by Epic Records, his role reduced to that of 'consultant'. I wish we had had the bravery to just stop and breathe and reflect but instead we steeled ourselves and donned our masks of brittle optimism and pushed onwards, responding to the ever-present need for 'momentum': music business-speak for a kind of blind panic, a condition that renders everyone infected bullish and myopic and temporarily bereft of wisdom. Also by this point we had wasted so much money on the album's meandering genesis via recording and re-recording that we couldn't afford not to release it, Suede Ltd needing the touring income and all of the other financial incentives that releasing records triggers. Of course it was a fatal error for us to put business decisions before the sanctity of our work, a mistake I have since vowed never to repeat, but to be brutally frank maybe by this point we sadly just didn't care enough.

After the drama of the last chapter it's hard not to make this final part feel slight and inconsequential. I have to admit that this is the episode of my career of which I am least proud and for which it feels that even the back story is slender and lightweight; a strangely incommensurate and underwhelming coda to a dramatic tale. There is only a small handful of songs of which I'm proud so it feels slightly silly going into detail about the birth of those pieces I feel don't deserve that respect. In many ways I wish we hadn't made this album. Even the artwork feels incongruous next to the visual narrative we had been carefully developing for a decade; a simplistic, featureless sort of logo image. Whereas previously we had created record covers that triggered our looming, polar themes of sensuality and sadness, the sleeve to *A New Morning* was soulless and blank and oddly corporate, bereft of any real personality or human content, perhaps a strangely appropriate reflection of the majority of the songs it clothed. Even though it now sounds bizarre, by the time it came to releasing it I simply had no idea what I really thought of the album and so, caught up in the grinding gears of practicality, we took that step of blind faith that you often need to bravely, and sometimes stupidly, make when releasing records and allowed it to be ushered out into the world much like a child wandering off into the traffic.

WHAT WILL SURVIVE
OF US IS LOVE

The mood in the back-stage dressing room of *The Graham Norton Show* was hushed and tense as we shuffled our way in and slumped heavily down on the plush chenille sofas. We were all lightly perspiring after the gestural pantomime that is a mimed TV appearance and so some of the band were cradling cold bottles of beer or sparkling water in crumpled plastic pint glasses and sipped them sullenly as I began to speak. My voice was quavering with the crushing emotion of the occasion that was being bizarrely juxtaposed by the underwhelmingly twee back-drop. This was the moment I had been rehearsing for over a year now. I had watched the band's inglorious, ignominious descent from a once proud beast to a wan, pallid invalid and now it was time to put it out of its misery. We owed it this respect, this final dignity. At last the words made their way out of my mouth: 'I can't do this any more,' I said, my voice sounding strange and high and shaky to my ears, 'it's over for Suede.' As with Neil's announcement to me a couple of years earlier I think the band immediately read into my flattened tone the solemnity and seriousness of what I was saying, and they knew that this was not the time for debate. I don't even remember adding much beyond that – possibly they had anticipated this moment, possibly they felt the same way. I think deep down, despite the upheaval to our lives, despite the hardship and the fear of stepping out into the unknown we all knew it was the kindest thing to do. We knew it was the right thing to do.

We had struggled on for a while, doing the kind of things bands do in the kind of places they do them and all the while behind the public mask I always wear I was wrestling with this torturous, torturous question. The band had become like a person to me: I had raised it and seen it grow and fed it and loved it and given it the best years of my life, and like a wonderful child it had given so much back to me and in turn seen me grow and without it my life would have been so different that I couldn't even conceive of it not existing. I felt a huge responsibility not just to Suede but to the members of Suede too, knowing that they had lives that would be massively affected by my decision but knowing too that they understood that a band must be so much more than a haven for stability. It must prowl and snarl and challenge and thrill and terrify and if it begins to fail to do these things then it relinquishes its right to protection. Towards the tail-end of the album campaign we had played some shows at the ICA that reflected on each of our records: a retrospective assessment of our time together that I had wanted to do as I felt it was an important closing gesture. During our performance of 'Saturday Night' at the *Coming Up* show I had felt an overwhelming flood of emotion as the song took me back to all of those wonderful early guileless years together and during the second verse, overcome with feeling, I began to cry. And so after all the drama of our turbulent, thrilling voyage – the dizzying highs, the desperate lows, the moments of dead-eyed stasis, the passion, the scruffy inelegant struggle, the savage beauty – we had arrived at the predictable end point at which all bands will eventually arrive. There's something so frustrating about inevitability – you think that you are immune to it and so to find yourself tripping and tumbling into the same traps that you assumed you would have had the nous to avoid takes on a second layer of distress. It feels like something or someone is mocking you, almost as if your failure is part of a hackneyed script and that your story, far from being unique, is just like all the others: one of youthful endeavour followed by a brief flicker of success and then the sour but familiar taste of defeat. Sadly it seems almost every band follows the same sort of career arc with the same points plotted grimly along the way like the Stations of the Cross: struggle, success, excess, disintegration and if you're lucky – enlightenment. We were after all no different, nothing special despite our ambitions and pretensions, and our time ended, like a thousand other bands before us and probably like a thousand other bands after us, in the same unhappy rat-run of dead ends and disillusionment and bitterness.

After all the sadness in these pages possibly the saddest part for me comes now. Charting the sorry, quiet collapse of a band that had once meant so much to so many is in a way a crueller fate than if we had exploded in a riot of notoriety and conflict. It was an ignoble end to a wonderful journey – a hushed finale completely out of keeping with the wild ride that had preceded it – but as I ruminate on the arc of our voyage and its muted denouement I understand that without it the band might possibly have never been reborn in the following decade with such spirit and élan and there might never have been the graceful closing act that was to come many years ahead. Sometimes it's not the sparkling moments that define us but the darker ones leading up to them.

CREDITS

'A Poison Tree', William Blake, *Songs of Experience* (1794)

Five Get into A Fix, Enid Blyton (Hodder and Stoughton, 1958)

The Wicker Man, directed by Robin Hardy and produced by Peter Snell (Studiocanal, 1973)

Platform, Michel Houellebecq (Vintage, 2003)

Excerpt from 'The Hawk in the Rain', Ted Hughes, *The Hawk in the Rain,* copyright © Estate of Ted Hughes (Faber & Faber, 1957) reprinted by kind permission of Faber & Faber and Farrar, Straus and Giroux

The Essential Martin Luther King, Jr: 'I Have a Dream' and Other Great Writings (Beacon Press, 2013)

Excerpts from 'Cut Grass' and 'An Arundel Tomb', *The Complete Poems of Philip Larkin*, Philip Larkin, edited by Archie Burnett, copyright © Estate of Philip Larkin (Faber & Faber, 2003) reprinted by kind permission of Faber & Faber and Farrar, Straus and Giroux

An Essay on Criticism, Alexander Pope (1711)

'Pearls Before Swine', Steve Sutherland, *Melody Maker*, 30 May 1992

The Quiet Ruin, Cattle in Water, A Sketch, Evening by J. M. W. Turner (exhibited 1809)

Charlie Watts, interview with David Hepworth, 1986

The Portrait of Dorian Gray, Oscar Wilde (Penguin Classics, 2012)